SIDDHARTHA

Hermann Hesse

Spark Educational Publishing
A Division of Barnes & Noble Publishing
120 Fifth Avenue
New York, NY 10011

ISBN 1-4114-0248-0

Please submit all comments and questions or report errors to *www.sparknotes.com/errors*

Printed and bound in the United States

INTRODUCTION:
STOPPING TO BUY SPARKNOTES ON A SNOWY EVENING

Whose words these are you *think* you know.
Your paper's due tomorrow, though;
We're glad to see you stopping here
To get some help before you go.

Lost your course? You'll find it here.
Face tests and essays without fear.
Between the words, good grades at stake:
Get great results throughout the year.

Once school bells caused your heart to quake
As teachers circled each mistake.
Use SparkNotes and no longer weep,
Ace every single test you take.

Yes, books are lovely, dark, and deep,
But only what you grasp you keep,
With hours to go before you sleep,
With hours to go before you sleep.

Contents

CONTEXT

Hermann Hesse was born in 1877 in the town of Calw, on the edge of Germany's Black Forest. He grew up in a missionary family whose religious beliefs deeply influenced him. His father was a Pietist-Lutheran who believed that humans are basically evil and need to be disciplined. Hesse's parents and grandparents had been missionaries in the Far East, however, and the spirituality and literature of Indians, Buddhists, and Middle Eastern cultures balanced Hesse's father's teachings.

Family and friends assumed that Hesse would one day become a member of the clergy, but Hesse did not take easily to the traditional teachings of the church. At the urging of his father, he entered the Maulbronn seminary at the age of fourteen but was soon expelled. A dark period followed, and Hesse experienced problems with severe depression and anger. Though he attempted to continue his studies, he had difficulty managing them. His teachers found him to be both precocious and rebellious, and he transferred schools several times, ultimately abandoning high school before finally graduating and returning to Calw. To make ends meet, Hesse took jobs working in bookstores. He spent much of his time at home with his father, where he read many of his grandfather's books on Eastern religion and philosophy. During this period he began to insinuate himself into Germany's circles of aspiring authors.

In 1904, at the age of thirty-seven, Hesse published his first novel, *Peter Camenzind*. A work that featured some unquestionably autobiographical content, Hesse's debut novel told the tale of an idealistic and driven youth who leaves his home in a Swiss mountain village to become a poet. Hesse's follow-up novel in 1906, *Unterm Rad*, also contained many autobiographical elements from Hesse's own adolescence. *Unterm Rad* is the story of a schoolboy who feels completely alienated from his contemporaries and flees from his school to travel through a variety of cities.

World War I galvanized Hesse as a political being and as an author. An avowed pacifist, Hesse joined the antiwar movement and plunged himself vigorously into writing antiwar novels and propaganda. He also edited two newspapers for German prisoners of war. But the war also sent him spiraling into a period of self-doubt and personal reflection. All of this took its toll on Hesse's private life, eventually leading to the breakup of his first marriage. Hesse meditated on the divorce, both indirectly and sometimes very directly, in the novels *Knulp* and *Rosshalde*. During this time, Hesse began studying the psychoanalytic works of Sigmund Freud. Excited by this relatively new discipline, Hesse voluntarily became a patient in a mental hospital and underwent psychiatric analysis with Freud's most famous prodigy, Carl Jung.

In 1919, after the war, Hesse moved permanently to Switzerland and published *Demian*. The novel, an instant commercial and critical success, reflects Hesse's fascination with Freud's conception of the subconscious and Jungian psychoanalysis, particularly Jung's description of "individuation," a process through which humans can become whole only by accepting both their conscious selves and their unconscious selves (such as their dreams and imagination). *Demian* also solidified Hesse's position as one of Europe's most eminent antiwar writers.

Throughout this time, Hesse remained interested in Eastern religions. Eager to learn more about new concepts of spirituality, he traveled several times to Asia and the Middle East. His studies eventually led to the publication of *Siddhartha* in 1922. This novel extended the themes already typical of Hesse's work: the alienation of man from man, the alienation of man from environment, and the desire for self-knowledge. In *Siddhartha*, however, Hesse explored these themes through a specifically Buddhist point of view. The novel was a success and quickly became Hesse's most famous book.

In 1927, Hesse wrote *Steppenwolf*, another major work that reflected not only Hesse's own spiritual journey but also a return to his consideration of modern political and social life in Germany. At this time, the seeds of World War II were being planted, and Hesse seemed keenly aware of the dangers of the fascist state about to grip Germany. *Steppenwolf* examines one man who is torn between his base animal impulses and his desire for social respectability, but it also portrays a Germany torn by anti-Semitism, poverty, and a crushing coldness of the soul.

The Glass Bead Game: (Magister Ludi), Hesse's last major work, was published in 1943. In this broad-ranging and very long book, which consists of several interconnected novels and novellas, Hesse continued to meditate upon the same themes of pacifism, Eastern religion, and the ultimate goal of self-knowledge and enlightenment. In the opening tale of *The Glass Bead*

Game, Hesse imagines a future in which academics and celibate priests have merged into a single entity, and in which the twentieth century has come to be known in retrospect as the century most famous for war in all of history.

In 1946, Hesse was awarded the Nobel Prize in literature. He lived the rest of his life quietly in Switzerland and died in 1962 at the age of eighty-five.

Plot Overview

Siddhartha, the handsome and respected son of a Brahmin, lives with his father in ancient India. Everyone in the village expects Siddhartha to be a successful Brahmin like his father. Siddhartha enjoys a near-idyllic existence with his best friend, Govinda, but he is secretly dissatisfied. He performs all the rituals of religion, and he does what religion says should bring him happiness and peace. Nonetheless, he feels something is missing. His father and the other elders have still not achieved enlightenment, and he feels that staying with them will not settle the questions he has about the nature of his existence. Siddhartha believes his father has already passed on all the wisdom their community has to offer, but he longs for something more.

One day, a group of wandering ascetics called Samanas passes through town. They are starved and almost naked and have come to beg for food. They believe enlightenment can be reached through asceticism, a rejection of the body and physical desire. The path the Samanas preach is quite different from the one Siddhartha has been taught, and he believes it may provide some of the answers he is looking for. He decides to follow this new path. Siddhartha's father does not want him to join the Samanas, but he cannot dissuade Siddhartha. Govinda also wants to find a path to enlightenment, and he joins Siddhartha in this new life.

Siddhartha adjusts quickly to the ways of the Samanas because of the patience and discipline he learned in the Brahmin tradition. He learns how to free himself from the traditional trappings of life, and so loses his desire for property, clothing, sexuality, and all sustenance except that required to live. His goal is to find enlightenment by eliminating his Self, and he successfully renounces the pleasures of the world.

Sunburned and half-starved, Siddhartha soon ceases to resemble the boy he used to be. Govinda is quick to praise the Samanas and notes the considerable moral and spiritual improvements they both have achieved since joining. Siddhartha, however, is still dissatisfied. The path of self-denial does not provide a permanent solution for him. He points out that the oldest Samanas have lived the life for many years but have yet to attain true spiritual enlightenment. The Samanas have been as unsuccessful as the Brahmins Siddhartha and

Govinda left behind. At this time, Siddhartha and the other Samanas begin to hear about a new holy man named Gotama the Buddha who has attained the total spiritual enlightenment called Nirvana. Govinda convinces Siddhartha they both should leave the Samanas and seek out Gotama. Siddhartha and Govinda inform the leader of the Samanas of their decision to leave. The leader is clearly displeased, but Siddhartha silences him with an almost magical, hypnotizing gaze.

Siddhartha and Govinda find Gotama's camp of followers and are taken in. Siddhartha is initially pleased with Gotama, and he and Govinda are instructed in the Eightfold Path, the four main points, and other aspects of Buddhism. However, while Govinda is convinced to join Gotama and his followers, Siddhartha still has doubts. He has noticed a contradiction in Gotama's teachings: Siddhartha questions how one can embrace the unity of all things, as the Buddha asks, if they are also being told to overcome the physical world. Siddhartha realizes Buddhism will not give him the answers he needs. Sadly, he leaves Govinda behind and begins a search for the meaning of life, the achievement of which he feels will not be dependent on religious instruction.

Siddhartha decides to embark on a life free from meditation and the spiritual quests he has been pursuing, and to instead learn from the pleasures of the body and the material world. In his new wanderings, Siddhartha meets a friendly ferryman, fully content with his simple life. Siddhartha crosses the ferryman's river and comes to a city. Here, a beautiful courtesan named Kamala entrances him. He knows she would be the best one to teach him about the world of love, but Kamala will not have him unless he proves he can fit into the material world. She convinces him to take up the path of the merchant. With her help, Siddhartha soon finds employment with a merchant named Kamaswami and begins to learn the trade. While Siddhartha learns the wisdom of the business world and begins to master the skills Kamaswami teaches him, Kamala becomes his lover and teaches him what she knows about love.

Years pass, and Siddhartha's business acumen increases. Soon, he is a rich man and enjoys the benefits of an affluent life. He gambles, drinks, and dances, and anything that can be bought in the material world is his for the taking. Siddhartha is detached from this life, however, and he can never see it as more than a game. He doesn't care if he wins or loses this game because it doesn't touch his spirit in any lasting way. The more he obtains in the material world, the less it satisfies him, and he is soon caught in a cycle of unhappiness that he tries to escape by engaging in even more gambling, drinking, and sex. When he is at his most disillusioned, he dreams that Kamala's rare songbird is dead in its cage. He understands that the material world is slowly killing him without providing him with the enlightenment for which he has been searching. One night, he resolves to leave it all behind and departs without notifying either Kamala or Kamaswami.

Sick at heart, Siddhartha wanders until he finds a river. He considers drowning himself, but he instead falls asleep on the riverbank. While he is sleeping, Govinda, who is now a Buddhist monk, passes by. Not recognizing Siddhartha, he watches over the sleeping man to protect him from snakes. Siddhartha immediately recognizes Govinda when he wakes up, but Govinda notes that Siddhartha has changed significantly from his days with the Samanas and now appears to be a rich man. Siddhartha responds that he is currently neither a Samana nor a rich man. Siddhartha wishes to become someone new. Govinda soon leaves to continue on his journey, and Siddhartha sits by the river and considers where his life has taken him.

Siddhartha seeks out the same content ferryman he met years before. The ferryman, who introduces himself as Vasudeva, radiates an inner peace that Siddhartha wishes to attain. Vasudeva says he himself has attained this sense of peace through many years of studying the river. Siddhartha expresses a desire to likewise learn from the river, and Vasudeva agrees to let Siddhartha live and work beside him. Siddhartha studies the river and begins to take from it a spiritual enlightenment unlike any he has ever known. While sitting by the river, he contemplates the unity of all life, and in the river's voice he hears the word Om.

One day Kamala the courtesan approaches the ferry along with her son on a pilgrimage to visit Gotama, who is said to be dying. Before they can cross, a snake bites Kamala. Siddhartha and Vasudeva tend to Kamala, but the bite kills her. Before she dies, she tells Siddhartha that he is the father of her eleven-year-old son. Siddhartha does his best to console and provide for his son, but the boy is spoiled and cynical. Siddhartha's son dislikes life with the two ferrymen and wishes to return to his familiar city and wealth. Vasudeva believes Siddhartha's son should be allowed to leave if he wants to, but Siddhartha is not ready to let him go. One morning, Siddhartha awakens to find his son has run away and stolen all of his and Vasudeva's money. Siddhartha chases after the boy, but as he reaches the city he realizes the chase is futile. Vasudeva follows Siddhartha and brings him back to their home by the river, instructing him to soothe the pain of losing his son by listening to the river.

Siddhartha studies the river for many years, and Vasudeva teaches Siddhartha how to learn the many secrets the river has to tell. In contemplating the river, Siddhartha has a revelation: Just as the water of the river flows into the ocean and is returned by rain, all forms of life are interconnected in a cycle without beginning or end. Birth and death are all part of a timeless unity. Life and death, joy and sorrow, good and evil are all parts of the whole and are necessary to understand the meaning of life. By the time Siddhartha has learned all the river's lessons, Vasudeva announces that he is through with his life at the river. He retires into the forest, leaving Siddhartha to be the ferryman.

The novel ends with Govinda returning to the river to seek enlightenment by meeting with a wise man who lives there. When Govinda arrives, he does not recognize that the wise man is Siddhartha himself. Govinda is still a follower of Gotama but has yet to attain the kind of enlightenment that Siddhartha now radiates, and he asks Siddhartha to teach him what he knows. Siddhartha explains that neither he nor anyone can teach the wisdom to Govinda, because verbal explanations are limited and can never communicate the entirety of enlightenment. Instead, he asks Govinda to kiss him on the forehead, and when Govinda does, the vision of unity that Siddhartha has experienced is communicated instantly to Govinda. Govinda and Siddhartha have both finally achieved the enlightenment they set out to find in the days of their youth.

CHARACTER LIST

Siddhartha The novel's protagonist. Siddhartha sets out on a quest for enlightenment and tests the religious philosophies he discovers. Siddhartha's most defining characteristic is his desire for a transcendent, spiritual understanding of himself and the world. He devotes himself wholeheartedly to the pursuit of this understanding, even when the path is difficult. Outside forces do not easily sway Siddhartha, and he follows his heart. A man dedicated to his personal quest for knowledge, Siddhartha will abandon a course if he feels it is flawed. Siddhartha has a son, who is also named Siddhartha.

Vasudeva The enlightened ferryman who guides Siddhartha to a transcendent understanding of himself and the universe. Vasudeva is spiritually and socially flawless, and he ferries true seekers of wisdom to enlightenment. He is closely linked to the river, and he helps Siddhartha learn how to listen to the river's secrets. Siddhartha achieves enlightenment only because of his association with Vasudeva.

Govinda Siddhartha's best friend and sometimes his follower. Like Siddhartha, Govinda devotes his life to the quest for understanding and enlightenment. He leaves his village with Siddhartha to join the Samanas, then leaves the Samanas to follow Gotama. He searches for enlightenment independently of Siddhartha but persists in looking for teachers who can show him the way. In the end, he is able to achieve enlightenment only because of Siddhartha's love for him.

Kamala A courtesan who instructs Siddhartha in the art of physical love. In addition to being Siddhartha's lover, Kamala helps him learn the ways of the city and leave his ascetic life as a Samana behind. Just before she dies from a snakebite, she reveals that Siddhartha is the father of her son.

8

Gotama   An enlightened religious leader with many followers. Also known as the Buddha, Gotama is said to have attained Nirvana. He teaches the Eightfold Path to his many followers as the way to achieve true enlightenment. Siddhartha and Govinda seek him out, but while Govinda becomes a follower, Siddhartha ultimately rejects him. Siddhartha concludes that while Gotama has achieved enlightenment, his teachings do not necessarily help others find enlightenment.

Kamaswami An older businessman who teaches Siddhartha the art of business. Kamala refers Siddhartha to Kamaswami, and with Kamaswami's guidance, Siddhartha successfully insinuates himself into the society of city-dwellers. Nonetheless, the lessons he learns from Kamaswami about the material world lead only to unhappiness. Money and business are just a game for Siddhartha, and they do not lead to fulfillment.

Young Siddhartha Siddhartha's son with Kamala. Young Siddhartha poses the final test Siddhartha must pass before enlightenment. When Kamala dies, young Siddhartha resists starting a new life with Siddhartha. He is a materialistic city-dweller, dislikes his father, and wants to return to his familiar city life. Siddhartha loves his son, and he must overcome this potentially binding love in order to achieve enlightenment. Just as Siddhartha's own father had to let him go out on his own, Siddhartha must let his son discover the world for himself.

Siddhartha's Father A respected Brahmin in Siddhartha's boyhood community. Siddhartha's father familiarizes Siddhartha with many basic religious teachings, but he is unable to provide Siddhartha with the answers he needs, which leads to Siddhartha's quest for enlightenment through other religious traditions. When the Samanas arrive to tempt Siddhartha away, Siddhartha's father initially resists but eventually lets him go.

The Samanas A group of traveling ascetics who believe that a life of deprivation and wandering is the path to self-actualization. The Samanas initially captivate Siddhartha and Govinda, but the two eventually forsake them to follow the teachings of Gotama. When Siddhartha eventually leaves the Samanas, he appears to have attained a superior level of spirituality.

ANALYSIS OF MAJOR CHARACTERS

SIDDHARTHA

An earnest spiritual pilgrim, Siddhartha is totally consumed by his quest for spiritual enlightenment. Though in his youth he learns the wisdom of his Brahmin heritage and masters the skills of the Samanas and the teachings of Gotama, the spiritual explanations that satisfy those around him are inadequate for Siddhartha because they do not lead to enlightenment. No matter how many others accept a particular religious explanation, Siddhartha will refuse the explanation if it rings false. Siddhartha seeks spiritual enlightenment at any cost, even when the search complicates other areas of life. Friends, lovers, and family members fall by the wayside when Siddhartha believes they are not compatible with his quest. Further, he believes no leader or philosophy is beyond questioning. Guided by a strong belief in his convictions, he argues with the head of the Samanas and even with the enlightened Gotama the Buddha himself. Siddhartha does not argue for argument's sake, nor does he question wisdom out of a sense of pride or superiority. He finds logical flaws in the teachings put before him, and he seeks the truth.

Siddhartha possesses an incredible degree of patience, which proves to be important since his quest takes a lifetime to fulfill. He progresses through successive spiritual explorations, experiences failure numerous times, but persists until he reaches his goal. The instantaneous, magical transmission of Nirvana from Siddhartha to Govinda demonstrates that Siddhartha has found the transcendent understanding they have both sought for so long. He has finally reached his goal.

Siddhartha is the Sanskrit name of the Buddha and means "he who is on the proper road" or "he who achieves his goal." Hesse is not attempting to directly portray the life of the Buddha himself through Siddhartha but to use Siddhartha as a means of discussing a path to enlightenment. At the same time, many striking similarities exist between Siddhartha and the actual Buddha. For example, both left promising lives in their pursuit of knowledge. In Siddhartha's case, he leaves Kamala when he becomes disillusioned with the material world, while the Buddha left a wife and son to become an ascetic. Both studied with ascetics, and both spent many years in study by a river, finally achieving enlightenment. Siddhartha has succeeded in his own arduous quest, and at the end of the novel, he is poised to take on followers of his own.

GOVINDA

Siddhartha's best friend, Govinda, is also an earnest spiritual pilgrim but does not question teachings to the same extent Siddhartha does. For example, though Govinda is excited at the chance to follow Gotama, Siddhartha goes along but says he has lost his faith in teachers. When Siddhartha decides to leave Gotama's side, Govinda instead remains stalwartly committed. Govinda does not choose his own path but follows the suggestions of others. Similarly, when the two old friends meet in the end, Govinda quickly apprentices himself to Siddhartha because Siddhartha has attained the Nirvana they both seek. The significant difference between Govinda and Siddhartha is that Govinda is primarily a follower, whereas Siddhartha is more inclined to strike out on his own path. This difference is one of the reasons Siddhartha is eventually able to achieve enlightenment through his own efforts, while Govinda needs assistance in order to achieve the same state. Siddhartha is better able to see the truth before him because of his self-reliance. Govinda needs others to point out the wisdom he should follow and is unable to see when he is following a flawed path and, ultimately, when he is nearing enlightenment.

At the beginning of their quest, when Govinda joins the Samanas, he may well have gone along simply to be with his friend. However, the severity and austere nature of their new lifestyle leaves little reason to doubt Govinda's conviction. He may be more of a follower than Siddhartha is, but his conviction and determination to find enlightenment are still strong. He does, after all, eventually find enlightenment, just as Siddhartha does—he just arrives at it in a different way.

VASUDEVA

Vasudeva, the enlightened ferryman, is the guide who finally leads Siddhartha to enlightenment. Siddhartha first meets Vasudeva after leaving Gotama and Govinda and immediately notices Vasudeva's serenity. Although Vasudeva lives within this world, his presence seems to transcend it, and all who meet him feel his divine, enlightened energy. He does not boast about his power or wisdom but simply credits all knowledge he has to the river. His primary action, other than ferrying passengers across the river, seems to be listening to whatever wisdom the river imparts to him. He is such a powerful figure that when a desperate, suicidal Siddhartha, convinced he'll never reach enlightenment, encounters Vasudeva a second time, he asks to become Vasudeva's apprentice. In a way, Siddhartha relies on Vasudeva to save his life.

Vasudeva does not teach Siddhartha a complicated philosophical belief system, only that he should learn from the river and allow it to explain its wisdom. Throughout Siddhartha's spiritual progression, Vasudeva keeps him moving in the right direction by prompting him to listen to the river whenever he has questions or doubts. In a bittersweet ending to their time together, Siddhartha's achievement of Nirvana coincides with the end of Vasudeva's time on the river and on earth. Vasudeva, who has literally and figuratively ferried Siddhartha to enlightenment, can now leave the earth, with Siddhartha taking over as ferryman. Vasudeva will live on in Siddhartha's own enlightenment and teachings.

Vasudeva is a name for Krishna, an incarnation of Vishnu, one of the powerful gods in a Hindu trinity, and means "he who lives in all thoughts, and who lives in all people." He is the most godlike figure within the book, yet he acts with surprising humility.

CHARACTER ANALYSIS

THEMES, MOTIFS, AND SYMBOLS

THEMES

Themes are the fundamental and often universal ideas explored in a literary work.

THE SEARCH FOR SPIRITUAL ENLIGHTENMENT

In *Siddhartha*, an unrelenting search for truth is essential for achieving a harmonious relationship with the world. The truth for which Siddhartha and Govinda search is a universal understanding of life, or Nirvana. Siddhartha and Govinda both have a fundamental desire to understand their lives through spirituality, seek to do this by reaching Nirvana, and start with the conviction that finding Nirvana is possible. Although Nirvana leads to a perfect relationship with the world and is thus an end goal that each man aspires to reach, Siddhartha and Govinda differ in what they're willing to do in search for this truth. In Siddhartha's case, when he becomes suspicious that one path may lead to a dead end, he quickly alters his course. He is willing to abandon the path of the Brahmins for the path of the Samanas, to leave the Samanas for Gotama, and then to make a radical departure from spiritual teachers and search in the material world with Kamala and Kamaswami. He does not relent in his search and instead continues to follow whatever path becomes available if he has clearly not yet reached Nirvana.

Govinda is much less flexible in his quest for spiritual enlightenment. In his quest, he restricts himself to the spiritual and religious world and persists in his need for teachers. Although Siddhartha is willing to break with religion itself and to abandon all his training, Govinda is willing to seek truth only as long as it appears within the narrow confines of Hinduism or Buddhism and is transmitted by a respected teacher. As a result, Govinda is unable to see the truth around him, since he is limited by his belief that truth will appear in the way he has been taught by his teachers. This distinction between Siddhartha's unrelenting search and Govinda's limited search is the reason why Govinda can attain enlightenment only through an act of grace on Siddhartha's part, whereas Siddhartha is able to find truth through his own powers.

INNER VS. EXTERIOR GUIDANCE

In *Siddhartha*, Siddhartha learns that enlightenment cannot be reached through teachers because it cannot be taught—enlightenment comes from within. Siddhartha begins looking for enlightenment initially by looking for external guidance from organized religion in the form of Brahmins, Samanas, and Buddhists. When these external spiritual sources fail to bring him the knowledge and guidance he needs, he discards them for Kamala and Kamaswami in the material world, again using an external source in his quest. These sources also fail to teach him wisdom, and he knows he must now find wisdom on his own. This realization itself comes from within. Siddhartha leaves the Brahmins, the Samanas, Gotama, and the material world because he feels dissatisfied, not because an external source tells him to go. His eventual attainment of Nirvana does not come from someone imparting the wisdom to him but instead through an internal connection to the river, which he finds contains the entire universe.

Vasudeva is a teacher of sorts for Siddhartha, and thus an external guide, but Vasudeva never attempts to tell Siddhartha what the meaning of life is. Instead, Vasudeva directs Siddhartha to listen to the river and search within himself for an understanding of what the river says. Vasudeva does not tell Siddhartha what the river will say, but when Siddhartha reveals what the river has told him, Vasudeva simply acknowledges that he too has received the same wisdom. The river itself never actually tells Siddhartha what its revelations mean. Instead, the river reveals the complexity of existence through sound and image, and Siddhartha meditates on these revelations in order to gain an understanding of them. Govinda, on the other hand, persists in looking to teachers for his wisdom, and in the end, asks Siddhartha to teach him the path to enlightenment. Because of this reliance on an external explanation, Govinda continuously fails to find Nirvana. His final success, however, does not come as explicit directions from Siddhartha on how to achieve enlightenment. Instead, Siddhartha acts as a conduit for Govinda, as the river did for him. He asks Govinda to kiss his forehead, an act that enables Govinda to see the nature of existence in an instant. Govinda's final revelation thus comes through his own interpretation of what Siddhartha shows him in the kiss. Though interior and exterior paths to enlightenment are both explored in *Siddhartha*, the exterior path is roundly rejected. Nirvana comes from within.

THE WISDOM OF INDIRECTION

Throughout the novel, Siddhartha pursues Nirvana differently, and though at first his tactics are aggressive and deliberate, he eventually finds that a more indirect approach yields greater rewards. Both Siddhartha and Govinda initially seek Nirvana aggressively and directly. Govinda remains dedicated to the relentless practice of Buddhist devotions that are specifically intended to bring about enlightenment, but Siddhartha eventually rejects these methods and instead relies on intuition for guidance. Siddhartha points out that by focusing only on the goal of Nirvana, Govinda failed to notice the tiny clues along the way that would have pointed him in the right direction. In effect, Govinda tries too hard. Siddhartha ultimately understands that because the essence of enlightenment already exists within us and is present in the world at every moment, prescriptive paths simply lead us further from ourselves and from the wisdom we seek. An indirect approach is more likely to take into account all elements of the world and is therefore better able to provide the necessary distance from which to see the unity of the world.

MOTIFS

Motifs are recurring structures, contrasts, or literary devices that can help to develop and inform the text's major themes.

LOVE

The role of love in Siddhartha's life changes throughout his search for enlightenment. The many ways love appears and the difficulties love poses are vital to the eventual success of Siddhartha's quest. Love first appears between Siddhartha and his father, a love Siddhartha rejects when he leaves his father to follow the Samanas. Love, at this stage, restricts Siddhartha's ability to realize spiritual wisdom, and he must abandon it. In the Buddha, Siddhartha sees love in action, primarily in the form of compassion, but Siddhartha rejects this love because it is part of teachings that do not lead him to enlightenment. Kamala teaches Siddhartha the physical aspects of love, as well as the importance of love itself. However, Siddhartha is incapable of giving and receiving genuine love at this stage. He has removed himself from the world so thoroughly that he is not motivated by what the world has to offer him.

With his son, Siddhartha finally feels love, but since love is an attachment to the world, it threatens to divert Siddhartha from his course. Until now, Siddhartha has gained wisdom in the absence of love, and the love he feels for his son becomes a test of this wisdom. Enlightenment cannot exist without love, and Siddhartha must accept love, painful as it might be, if he is to achieve Nirvana. Through Kamala and his son he has learned to love the world and accept it, not resist it, in its entirety.. Siddhartha is a part of the world, yet at the same time he can transcend it.

OM

The concept of Om, which signifies the oneness and unity of all things, marks key moments of awakening for Siddhartha. Siddhartha's ability to finally comprehend Om is his entrance into enlightenment, but along the way he encounters the idea a number of times, each time sparking a change within him. He first encounters Om in his training as a Brahmin. He realizes that though he has been taught what Om should mean, none of those around him have fully achieved an understanding of it in their own lives. People who chant the word and understand the concept intellectually surround him, but their lives do not reflect the enlightenment that comes from fully embracing the energy of Om. He hears Om again when he stands near the river contemplating suicide. Realizing that life itself is indestructible, he must learn to just "be," not try to force his life along specific paths. Essentially, he is trying to merge with Om, which he recognizes as being all around him, rather than continuously search for a philosophy that accesses it on an intellectual basis. At the end of the novel, the more he listens to the river, the more aware he becomes of the complexity of Om and how it involves not only the physical and spiritual world but also time itself. When he finally comprehends the word in its entirety and understands that all things exist at the same moment, all possibilities are real and valid, and time itself is meaningless, he finally achieves enlightenment.

POLARITIES

In *Siddhartha*, Siddhartha finds that enlightenment does not come from mastering either the material or spiritual world but from finding the common ground between these polarities of existence. In the first third of the book, Siddhartha rejects the material world. The Brahmins, Samanas, and Buddhists all maintain that the material

MOTIFS

world is illusion, or Maya, that distracts a seeker from the spiritual truth. Adopting this belief, Siddhartha completely denies his body and, instead, focuses his efforts on refining his mind and memorizing the knowledge his teachers pass along to him. In the second third of the book, Siddhartha rejects the spiritual world and enters the material world, but relentlessly pursuing carnal desire does not lead him to wisdom either. Siddhartha battles with other polar opposites as well, such as time/timelessness and attachment/detachment, but in these, too, he finds that embracing one and rejecting the other does not lead to enlightenment. The river suggests this battle visually: the opposing banks represent the polarities, and the river itself represents the ideal union of them. Siddhartha finds enlightenment only when he understands Om, the unity of polarities. He achieves transcendence when he can accept that all is false and true at the same time, that all is living and dead at the same moment, and that all possibilities are united in the spirit of the universe.

SYMBOLS

Symbols are objects, characters, figures, or colors used to represent abstract ideas or concepts.

THE RIVER
The river in *Siddhartha* represents life itself, time, and the path to enlightenment. As a representation of life, it provides knowledge without words, and Siddhartha's reward for studying it is an intuitive understanding of its divine essence. The river's many sounds suggest the sounds of all living things, and the flow of the river, as well as the fact that its water perpetually returns, suggests the nature of time. The ferryman points Siddhartha in the right direction, but the river itself is Siddhartha's final instructor.

THE FERRYMAN
In *Siddhartha*, the ferryman is a guide for both the river and the path to enlightenment. The ferryman is positioned between ordinary world and enlightenment, and those who seek enlightenment and are open to guidance will find what they need within the ferryman. Many teachers of wisdom appear during Siddhartha's search, but each fails to lead Siddhartha to enlightenment. The ferryman, however, shows Siddhartha how to find enlightenment within himself. The first time Vasudeva meets Siddhartha, Siddhartha wants only to

cross the river, and that is all Vasudeva helps him do. Vasudeva is not a teacher who will simply tell Siddhartha what he should know, but a guide who will lead him where he wishes to go. Years later, Siddhartha searches for knowledge from the river itself, and Vasudeva guides him in his attempts to hear what the river has to say. Siddhartha himself becomes a ferryman after he reaches enlightenment. He guides people back and forth across the river and eventually helps Govinda find enlightenment. In *Siddhartha*, only the ferrymen are able to help others find enlightenment.

THE SMILE

The only characters in *Siddhartha* who smile are those who have achieved enlightenment, and the smile evokes their spiritual perfection and harmony. Smiles are scarce among the Hindus and Samanas and in the material world, since enlightenment cannot be faked or forced. Only after going through the requisite stages leading to enlightenment can one express the beatific smile. Siddhartha first sees the smile in Gotama. The smile evokes Gotama's saintliness and peace, and it impresses Siddhartha. Even when Siddhartha argues with him, Gotama responds with a smile, indicating the balance of an enlightened soul. Similarly, the smile marks Vasudeva as an enlightened soul, and he too impresses Siddhartha with his peaceful state. Vasudeva often smiles rather than talks, suggesting that enlightenment is communicated without words. Siddhartha himself does not exhibit a smile until he has achieved his own enlightenment, and this smile, in part, enables Govinda to realize that Siddhartha is like Gotama.

SYMBOLS

SUMMARY AND ANALYSIS

PART ONE

> *"You will grow tired, Siddhartha."*
> *"I will grow tired."*
> *"You will fall asleep, Siddhartha."*
> *"I will not fall asleep."*
> *"You will die, Siddhartha."*
> *"I will die."*
> (See QUOTATIONS, p. 48)

SUMMARY: THE BRAHMIN'S SON

The novel is set six centuries before the birth of Christ, in ancient India at the time of Gotama the Buddha, whose Eightfold Path guides the faithful toward Nirvana. Siddhartha is a young Brahmin, handsome and learned, with the potential to be a prince among his caste members. Everyone knows he is destined for greatness because he has mastered all the rituals and wisdom of his religion at an early age. His village is idyllic, and Siddhartha seems to live an enviable life. His father is a Brahmin, a religious leader and esteemed member of the community. Siddhartha seems well on his way to following in his father's footsteps.

Though Siddhartha spends his time studying the Hindu wisdom of his elders along with his best friend Govinda, he is dissatisfied. He suspects that his father and the other erudite Brahmins have learned perfectly everything from the holy books, but he does not believe they have achieved enlightenment. The rituals and mantras they have taught him seem more a matter of custom than a real path that could lead to true enlightenment. To become religious men by the standards of their own community, Siddhartha feels he and Govinda would have to become like sheep in a large herd, following predetermined rituals and patterns without ever questioning those methods or exploring methods beyond the ones they know. Siddhartha is deeply unhappy at this prospect. Though he loves his father and respects the people of his village, he cannot imagine himself existing in this way. Siddhartha has followed his father's example with conviction, but still he longs for something more.

One evening after meditating, Siddhartha announces to Govinda that he will join a group of Samanas, wandering mendicant priests, who have just passed through their city. The Samanas are starved, half-naked, and must beg for food, but only because they believe enlightenment can be reached through asceticism, a rejection of the body and physical desire. The Samanas seem completely different from the religious elders in Siddhartha's own community, and since he has not found the wisdom he has been searching for at home, he decides he should follow the Samanas' path and see what he can learn from them. When Siddhartha informs Govinda that he will join the Samanas, Govinda is frightened. He knows Siddhartha is taking his first step into the world and that Govinda himself must follow.

Siddhartha, a dutiful son, asks his father for permission before leaving with the Samanas. His father is disappointed and says he does not want to hear the question a second time, but Siddhartha does not move. The father cannot sleep and gets up every hour to find Siddhartha standing with crossed arms in the darkness. In the morning, his father reluctantly gives permission. He knows Siddhartha will not change his mind. He asks that Siddhartha return home to teach his father the art of bliss if he finds it elsewhere. As he leaves to join the wandering Samanas, Siddhartha is pleased and surprised to learn that Govinda has decided to join him in this new life outside the village.

ANALYSIS: THE BRAHMIN'S SON

Despite his solid spiritual upbringing among the Brahmins, Siddhartha still seeks the meaning of life, and he embarks on a quest to find enlightenment. Brahmins are members of the highest of the four interdependent groups, called castes, that make up Hindu society. Members of the Brahmin caste were originally priests with the primary duty of mediating with and praying to gods, and they were respected for their intellect and their knowledge of the Vedas, the sacred Hindu religious texts. In "The Brahmin's Son," Siddhartha meditates on the syllable Om, which represents perfection and unity. Om suggests the holy power that animates everything within and around us. This power does not have form or substance, but it is the source of everything that was, is, and will be. For Siddhartha, finding perfect fulfillment on earth requires understanding Om and gaining unity with it. Siddhartha understands what Om means, but he has not yet merged with it, and has therefore not reached enlightenment. Siddhartha's quest is a quest for true understanding of Om, and his quest will lead him far from home and through several paths of wisdom before he can reach his spiritual goal.

Hesse modeled Siddhartha on the Buddha, and the lives of the two figures are similar in many ways. Siddhartha's name itself is the first suggestion of the link between Siddhartha and the Buddha, for the historical Buddha, Gotama Sakyamuni, also bore the given name Siddhartha. In *Siddhartha*, Siddhartha's life parallels the little that is known of the Buddha's history. Buddha's life was formed around three seminal events: the departure from his father's house, the wasted and frustrating years torn between the pursuit of worldly desires and a life of extreme asceticism, and, finally, the determination of the Middle Path as the only road to enlightenment. Siddhartha also follows this course throughout the novel. He leaves his father, explores several kinds of spiritual teachings, and eventually achieves enlightenment. In this way, Siddhartha resembles the original Buddha, both seeker and sage.

The divisions of *Siddhartha* correspond to the Buddha's doctrine. The first four chapters evoke the Four Noble Truths, which are the Buddha's basic teachings and concern the necessity of suffering in life, and the next eight chapters evoke the Eightfold Path, which details how to end the suffering described in the Four Noble Truths. Buddha's First Noble Truth, that life means suffering, is revealed to Siddhartha while he is still a son of the Brahmins, living in his father's house. Ritual and formula govern Siddhartha's father's world. Life in this world revolves around sacrifices and offerings made at certain times and the performance of established duties that everyone, even Siddhartha's father, must take part in. The father's world, then, is fixed in the moment and regulated according to certain accepted guidelines. Nothing will change from one day to the next. Siddhartha's father's request at the end of this chapter that Siddhartha return home to teach his father if he is successful is an admission that Siddhartha is right, that the gods are only objects of veneration and not living companions. The people in this world suffer from a way of life that was forced on them, and their strict rituals and schedules stand between them and the reality they seek.

> *He lost his Self a thousand times and for days on end he*
> *dwelt in non-being. But although the paths took him*
> *away from Self, in the end they always led back to it.*
> *(See* QUOTATIONS, *p. 49)*

SUMMARY: WITH THE SAMANAS

Siddhartha and Govinda begin wandering with the Samanas. They quickly adopt the ways of their new teachers, dressing in rags and taking only the barest sustenance necessary to preserve life. Soon, Siddhartha and Govinda adopt the starved and beaten appearance shared by the other Samanas. The philosophy behind the Samanas' way of life is the belief that true enlightenment comes when the Self is destroyed or completely negated. They direct their ascetic practices towards this central goal. Once Siddhartha has joined the Samanas, his only goal is to become empty of everything, including wishes, dreams, joy, and passion. Siddhartha reasons that after he has destroyed every impulse in his heart, his innermost being will surely awaken.

Siddhartha embraces these new practices and teachings and quickly adjusts to the way of the Samanas because of the patience and discipline he had learned while studying Hinduism with his father. He soon learns how to be free of the traditional trappings of life, losing his desire for property, clothing, sexuality, and all sustenance except that required to live. His goal is to find enlightenment by eliminating his Self, and he is able to successfully renounce the pleasures of the world and the desires of the Self. He becomes a protégé of the eldest Samana, but the deepest secret remains hidden, and Siddhartha eventually realizes that destroying the will is not the answer. While both Siddhartha and Govinda enjoy substantial spiritual advancement during their time with the Samanas, Siddhartha doubts that this way of life will provide him with the ultimate spiritual Nirvana he seeks. The path of self-denial does not provide a permanent solution for him. He shares his misgivings with Govinda, arguing that the eldest of the Samanas is sixty years old and still has not attained enlightenment, and that the Samanas have been no more successful than the Brahmins Siddhartha and Govinda left behind. Govinda disagrees and points out the considerable spiritual progress they have both made. Though Govinda's counterarguments do not sway Siddhartha, they both remain with the Samanas.

After Siddhartha and Govinda have been with the Samanas for three years, a rumor reaches them that an enlightened one, Gotama the Buddha, has appeared, someone who has overcome the suffering of the world and has brought his chain of karma, or rebirth, to an end. Some are skeptical of these reports, including the senior Samanas, but the news excites Siddhartha and Govinda. Govinda yearns to follow this new master, and Siddhartha agrees they should seek him out, although he has lost faith in teachers. Siddhartha uses Gotama as a means of finally extricating Govinda from the sway of the Samanas. The two friends resolve to find Gotama and follow him. The Samana elder is angry when Siddhartha announces their departure, but Siddhartha hypnotizes the Samana with his gaze, utterly silencing him. The old man silently backs away and blesses him. As Siddhartha and Govinda leave together for Gotama's camp, Govinda observes that Siddhartha's mesmerizing gaze proves he has attained a spirituality higher than that of the highest Samana.

ANALYSIS: WITH THE SAMANAS

Siddhartha hopes the Samanas' asceticism will help him break free of the cycle of time that was so binding in his father's world, but asceticism succeeds only in revealing the second of Buddha's Four Noble Truths: The cause of suffering is the craving for something that can never be satisfied. The Samanas believe that enlightenment can be found only through the denial of flesh and worldly desires. Siddhartha tries to escape from time, to become a void, and in so doing create an empty space that only the unified power of the universe will be able to fill. Hard as Siddhartha tries to escape from himself and his reality, however, he always returns to a Self that is restricted by time, and he realizes that asceticism will not bring salvation. He cannot escape the problem of time just because he wills himself to. His attempts to escape from suffering lead only to further suffering, and the denial of time roots him even more firmly in the cycle of time. He has learned that timelessness cannot be found apart from the Self, rendering the Samanas' teaching useless for him.

The Samanas' teachings aim to enable the seeker of knowledge to escape the physical world, but Siddhartha discovers that true enlightenment cannot come from ignoring the world around him. He explains to Govinda that what the Samanas do is no different from what a drunkard does: They escape the Self temporarily. Just as the drunkard continues to suffer and does not find enlightenment even though he continually escapes the body, the Samanas are trapped on a path that offers temporary escape from suffering but does not lead to enlightenment. As soon as the Samanas cease their spiritual practices, the real world comes rushing back, and whatever enlightenment has been achieved dissipates. Since Siddhartha is searching for a permanent answer, he cannot follow the Samanas. He understands that true enlightenment can come only when the approach used to reach it takes into account the world itself.

The confrontation between Siddhartha and the elder Samana suggests that enlightenment cannot come from teachers but must be realized within, a fact Siddhartha will discover repeatedly on his quest. Siddhartha leaves the Hinduism of his father because of its flaws, just as he leaves the teachings of the Samanas because they do not lead him to enlightenment. Siddhartha encounters resistance when he tries to leave both his father and the Samanas, but in both cases he leaves with their blessings, which suggests that these elders are in error and that Siddhartha's path is justified. Teachers may not be able to give Siddhartha enlightenment, but they do, in their own ways, set him on a path that will help him find enlightenment for himself. Although Siddhartha looked to both instructors for knowledge of enlightenment, both fail to give him what he needs, and Siddhartha realizes that these paths will not lead him to the enlightenment he seeks.

Despite the flaws Siddhartha finds with the Samanas' teachings, his interaction with them is essential to his quest for enlightenment, since through them he realizes that enlightenment must not discount the physical world. Siddhartha's Brahmin upbringing led him to search for an enlightenment based purely in spiritual knowledge, specifically the idea of a universal force, Om. With the Samanas, Siddhartha experiences his most purely spiritual existence to date, but his failure to achieve enlightenment suggests to him that enlightenment cannot be a purely spiritual. The material world consistently intrudes, and Siddhartha must take it into account as he continues his search. Though the Samanas' path does not lead to the enlightenment Siddhartha seeks, it does lead to an essential revelation that enables him to eventually find enlightenment. Without the Samanas, Siddhartha may have continued in his purely spiritual pursuits, perpetually removing himself from the physical world and failing to reach his goal. Though the Samanas don't lead him to enlightenment, they help him eliminate the purely spiritual path, thereby leading him closer to finding a path to success.

The mesmerizing gaze Siddhartha gives the Samana elder is never explained in the text, but the fact that Siddhartha apparently has a certain power over the Samana suggests that he is already spiritually superior. Not only did the Samanas not lead Siddhartha to enlightenment, but Siddhartha is closer to it than they are, even if neither he nor the Samanas realize it yet. Siddhartha's gaze renders the Samana speechless, which facilitates Siddhartha's departure. Just as he steadfastly waited in his father's room when he wanted to leave the Brahmins, he gazes steadily here to obtain his goal. This gaze seems magical, but it also suggests something very real and human: Siddhartha's astonishing strength of will and unwavering determination to reach enlightenment.

> [T]here is one thing that this clear, worthy instruction does not contain; it does not contain the secret of what the Illustrious One himself experienced—he alone among hundreds of thousands.
>
> *(See* QUOTATIONS, *p. 50)*

SUMMARY: GOTAMA

Siddhartha and Govinda journey to the camp of Gotama's followers, and the followers welcome them as spiritual pilgrims. Gotama makes a deep impression on Siddhartha and Govinda. He seems to radiate pure enlightenment. His teachings include Buddhism's Eightfold Path, the Fourfold Way, and other aspects of Buddhism, as well as many practices similar to those of the Samanas. Siddhartha and Govinda dedicate themselves to these teachings. Govinda quickly resolves to give himself over completely to the lifestyle Gotama prescribes. However, while Govinda is completely swayed by Gotama and decides to join his followers permanently, Siddhartha has doubts and finds he has trouble completely accepting some of Gotama's teachings.

The next morning, when Siddhartha unexpectedly meets Gotama in the grove, he boldly speaks to him about his doctrine, praising his victory in finding the unbroken chain of being, of cause and effect. For Siddhartha, however, the unity is imperfect. The message cannot contain for Siddhartha, or for others, the secret of what Gotama himself has experienced. Siddhartha also points out a contradiction to Gotama: How can one embrace the unity of all things, as Gotama asks, if they are also told to overcome the physical world?

Gotama responds that his goal is not to give a perfect mathematical understanding of the universe, but to achieve freedom from suffering. Siddhartha responds that while Gotama himself has achieved Nirvana, he did it on his own, without a teacher. Siddhartha implicitly questions the efficacy of the approach prescribed by Gotama to his followers. Gotama admits that Siddhartha may technically have a point but also notes that Siddhartha can put forward no spiritual guidance superior to his own. Gotama asks if, according to Siddhartha's reasoning, his legions of followers would not be better off pursuing a life of pleasure in the city. Siddhartha leaves his meeting with Gotama unconvinced that Gotama's way of life is right for him. Sadly, he also leaves Govinda behind and begins a search for a way to find the meaning of life that is not dependent on religious instruction.

ANALYSIS: GOTAMA

Although Siddhartha has been looking for someone to show him the path to enlightenment, his meeting with Gotama convinces him that no formula for salvation or enlightenment can exist. Just as the Hindus and Samanas that Siddhartha left behind preached a specific route to enlightenment, Gotama similarly teaches a set of rules. His rules, like those of the Hindus and Samanas, speak of renunciation as a means of escaping suffering. However, Siddhartha has already realized during his time with the Samanas that he cannot reach enlightenment by rejecting the world of the Self and the world of the body. He cannot believe in Nirvana if it means separation from life's suffering. By leaving Gotama, Siddhartha rejects the prescribed formula for reaching enlightenment that this religion offers. Siddhartha realizes that all religions offer specific formulas for reaching enlightenment, just as all teachers offer knowledge couched in terms of their own experiences, and so he cannot rely on any individual religion or teacher in his search for enlightenment.

Neither Gotama nor any other guide can teach enlightenment because wisdom must be learned through experience, and it cannot be communicated through words. Gotama's lectures communicate knowledge about enlightenment and what causes suffering, but the listener cannot translate this knowledge into actual enlightenment. The knowledge leads to greater understanding, but words themselves cannot substitute for experience, and their meaning depends on usage and interpretation. Though Gotama speaks of enlightenment, his efforts can enable a follower only to realize that the possibility of enlightenment exists—he cannot provide enlightenment itself. The follower must experience the revelation for himself or herself, which in a way renders a teacher useless: the process of reaching enlightenment is internal. Siddhartha knows this already, so he cannot become one of Gotama's followers.

SUMMARY & ANALYSIS

Govinda remains behind in order to follow Gotama, and although Siddhartha is saddened by his departure, he also understands that he must seek enlightenment alone. Because formulas for enlightenment do not exist, and teachers cannot pass enlightenment on to their students, Siddhartha must seek enlightenment by searching his own soul alone. Gotama has followers, but he has already achieved enlightenment and can endure distractions. Siddhartha, however, has not yet achieved enlightenment and is distracted by Govinda's presence. He will be unable to achieve enlightenment as long as Govinda remains with him, so he lets Govinda go. Only when Govinda leaves is Siddhartha free to truly test himself in the manner necessary to bring about enlightenment.

SUMMARY: AWAKENING

When Siddhartha leaves the grove, he is done with teachers and teaching. He wants to know himself, learn from himself, and understand himself. He feels as though he is seeing the world, puzzling and magical, for the first time. He realizes he is in the middle of the world and that he is not enlightened, but that he can awaken while learning more about himself. Siddhartha is suddenly infused with a powerful certainty in his own powers of self-realization. He feels he has truly become a man. He believes his path to Nirvana will not come from following another person's prescriptive lifestyle. Instead, Siddhartha feels sure that his path to enlightenment will come from within himself. Thus resolved, his new task will be to discover how to find this enlightenment. His first impulse is to return home to his father, but then he realizes that his home is part of the past. He suddenly knows he is completely alone, and a shudder runs through him.

ANALYSIS: AWAKENING

In "Awakening," Siddhartha fully understands that discovery and enlightenment must come through the world of the here and now. Siddhartha suddenly sees the world's beauty and realizes that meaning is everywhere. Here, in the midst of what exists within him and around him, Siddhartha must discover who and what he is. He calls this discovery a rebirth, one of several rebirths he will undergo during his quest. This rebirth signifies the death of what he was and his ignorance of what he will become. He knows he cannot return to his father because he will not gain any more wisdom from the past. He is also aware that he does not know where he'll end up. In a way, this moment exists independently of the rest of time: briefly, Siddhartha has no remembered past and no discernible future. This moment in the present marks more than a transition, however, because it offers Siddhartha a glimpse of the sum of all individual instants in time. Although Siddhartha barely realizes it, this supreme awareness brings him close to the unity he seeks.

"Awakening" encapsulates the revelation Siddhartha has learned from his experiences in the preceding chapters: Enlightenment cannot be reached by relying on teachers or by ignoring the world. This chapter marks the end of one phase of Siddhartha's quest. The next part of his quest must take him away from the spiritual world and into the material world. Although Siddhartha had considered the freedoms and limitations of the spiritual and material worlds in earlier chapters, he contemplates them more fully here. Since these thoughts end Part One, and since Siddhartha has an actual moment of enlightenment in the middle of the chapter, we can assume that these considerations prompt Siddhartha's greater understanding of self. "Awakening" gathers the import of the first few chapters, crystallizes them within Siddhartha's mind, and shows how they act as catalyst for revelation, prompting Siddhartha to move forward into the material world. He can no longer ignore the material world. His imminent investigation of the material world, and the knowledge he'll gain from this investigation, will be just as important as the knowledge he has gained thus far from his association with teachers and religion.

The conclusion to "Awakening" suggests that Siddhartha's upcoming investigation into the material world is a continuation of a correct path toward enlightenment. Siddhartha knows what he seeks and is aware of when he moves toward it or remains static in one stage of development. Although he feels a moment of despair about his solitude, he continues with renewed vigor. The lessons he has learned are clear in his mind, he sees the world in its beauty, and he is energized to move forward. Although he does not have a clear sense of how he'll achieve his enlightenment, he is confident that he will find his way through his own direction. The heightened moment of lyricism in the middle of the chapter seemingly bolsters Siddhartha's confidence. Through this lyrical writing, Hesse conveys to the reader that Siddhartha's optimism is correct, and that the next steps will bring him closer to his goal.

PART TWO

SUMMARY: KAMALA

For a time Siddhartha wanders aimlessly. He sees the physical world with fresh eyes, noticing the animals that frolic around him and the beautiful plants along his path. For the first time he truly feels a part of the present and notices the world as it is, rather than ignoring it in favor of more spiritual, abstract contemplations. He spends the first night of his new life in a ferryman's hut and dreams of Govinda. In the dream, Govinda, imitating Christ, asks, "Why hast thou forsaken me?" Then Govinda changes into a woman, and Siddhartha suckles at her breast.

The next day Siddhartha asks the ferryman to take him across the river. The ferryman tells Siddhartha he has learned much from the river, and Siddhartha finds comfort in the ferryman's words. When they reach the other bank, Siddhartha regrets not being able to pay the ferryman, but the ferryman does not seem to mind. He prophesies that Siddhartha will return to the river in the future, and that Siddhartha will give him a gift at that time.

At the edge of a village, a young woman appears and attempts to seduce Siddhartha. Though she tempts him, his inner voice tells him to resist. However, the next woman Siddhartha sees as he enters the city offers a temptation he can't resist. She is Kamala, a beautiful, elegant courtesan. As her sedan chair is carried past Siddhartha, she returns his smile. His first worldly goal is clear.

After a bath in the river and a haircut and shave from a friendly barber, Siddhartha returns to Kamala. She is amused that a Samana should come out of the forest and ask to be taught the art of love. Even though she is willing to exchange a kiss for a poem, he will learn no more until he can return wearing fine clothes and bearing gifts. Despite her apparent amusement, she recommends Siddhartha to her friend Kamaswami, a wealthy businessman, but insists that Siddhartha become his equal, not his servant.

ANALYSIS: KAMALA

The title of this chapter, "Kamala," and those of the two chapters that follow suggest that Siddhartha will seek meaning in the world of the senses, a radical departure from his exploration of the spiritual world. The root word of Kamala, *kama*, signifies the Hindu god of love and desire. Siddhartha's immersion in this world will awaken these aspects of himself, which he has long kept quiet. His transformation begins even before he meets Kamala or Kamaswami. His increased awareness of the sensory world, apparent from the beginning of this chapter, demonstrates that he is allowing the world to influence him. In the past, he trained himself to deny the senses and find the truth by ignoring the world and time, which he took to be illusory. This idea of the world as illusion, or *Maya*, is common to Hindu and Buddhist philosophy and suggests that the material world is a distraction from the divine, essential truth. By trying to see the world with clarity, rather than ignoring it as Maya, Siddhartha has made a clear break from his previous spiritual understanding.

Siddhartha's dream of Govinda turning into a woman marks a transitional moment in Siddhartha's life, as he moves away from his previous ascetic life that he shared with Govinda toward a new life of desire, which he'll share with Kamala. Initially, this shift concerns mainly Siddhartha's senses and imagination, but his encounter with the washerwoman at the edge of the village makes him consider if and when he will enter the world of desire. He rejects her, despite desiring her, which indicates an awareness of the difference between obeying one's inner voice and succumbing to impulse. When Siddhartha becomes Kamala's lover, he makes a conscious choice to enter the world of desire, and he becomes attached to it.

Siddhartha's encounters with the two women suggest that physical desire and sex are essential aspects of the material world he must explore. When the first woman wordlessly invites Siddhartha to engage in a sexual act, Siddhartha refuses her, but his curiosity about sex remains. When he sees the beautiful courtesan Kamala, his lust finds a focal point. When Siddhartha decides to make sex his new project, he immerses himself with an intensity usually reserved for his religious apprenticeship. Although he has rejected spiritual teachers, he will accept a teacher of desire, and he consciously decides to follow her teachings. Siddhartha is not an innocent, and neither is he willing to passively accept whatever sexual experience falls into his lap. He is, to some extent, calculating and ambitious. He asks around about Kamala, and when he speaks with her, his deep commitment to change himself to obtain her love becomes apparent to both of them. Siddhartha completes the break from the spiritual world when he shaves and has his hair trimmed, for he has finally taken into account his own physical body, transforming himself in order to fit into the material world.

SUMMARY: AMONGST THE PEOPLE

Kamaswami agrees to receive Siddhartha in his home, but he is suspicious about what Siddhartha can do for him. Siddhartha follows Kamala's advice and does not beg for work but, instead, acts in a manner that requires Kamaswami to treat him respectfully. Kamaswami quizzes Siddhartha about his desire to become a businessman, not expecting much. When Siddhartha answers honestly, and shows that he can read and write, Kamaswami is impressed and offers to take Siddhartha as a protégé. Siddhartha lives in Kamaswami's house and works with him as a merchant. Siddhartha handles the business world with relative ease, but he does not emotionally attach himself to the results of his ventures, laughing off failure as easily as he laughs at his success. Disturbed by this flippant attitude, Kamaswami tries to motivate Siddhartha by giving him a small percentage of the gains from each transaction. Yet business remains only a game for Siddhartha, and nothing Kamaswami does can make him take business affairs more seriously. Kamaswami suggests that he try giving himself over to the pleasures wealth can bring, but still Siddhartha does not change his perspective. His life as a Samana showed him that many people live in a childish, animalistic way, suffering over things that have little real meaning, such as money, pleasure, and honor. Siddhartha rejects this sort of suffering.

Kamala, on the other hand, opens Siddhartha to the world of love, which excites him far more than the merchant life Kamaswami offers. Siddhartha works hard with Kamaswami in order to afford the gifts and clothes necessary to court Kamala, but he feels he learns far more important lessons from her than from Kamaswami. He learns much about the physical act of love, but also about patience and self-respect. He notes that she understands him better than do Govinda or Kamaswami, because she, unlike Kamaswami, can always retreat from the material world and be herself. Her life seems to have purpose and meaning and in this way seems similar to the life of Gotama himself.

Though they share great intimacy and a feeling of connection, Siddhartha and Kamala are not in love. For Kamala, sex is a part of her work as a courtesan, and her instruction of Siddhartha is undertaken primarily for financial gain. Similarly, Siddhartha is interested in his relationship with Kamala only because it provides him deeper insights into the world of love that might better enable him to achieve enlightenment. Though Siddhartha is the best lover Kamala has ever had, Kamala and Siddhartha realize that people like themselves cannot truly love.

ANALYSIS: AMONGST THE PEOPLE

Siddhartha's decision to exploit the senses, instead of denying them, draws him into the world of time and average people. This world is linked to the Hindu god *Kama*, the god of desires, who is represented in the names of those closest to him during this period: Kamala and Kamaswami. From these worldly people, Siddhartha learns much that is useful in the world of time, including how to live happily in the moment and induce it to yield its fruits, as well as how to use the present to produce a desired consequence in the future. Yet at the same time, and almost without his knowing it, Siddhartha's life in the world of Kama brings him the first of those virtues appropriate to a seeker of enlightenment. From Kamala he learns part of the Eightfold Path considered "right attitude," which indicates that the correct way to approach an experience is to completely surrender the Self while keeping the purpose steadily in mind. In addition, from Kamaswami he learns the concept of "right aspiration," which indicates that working for an immediate gain yields no real profit. Kamaswami actually exemplifies the opposite of this concept, and his failure enables Siddhartha to realize that only a voluntary investment can give a worthwhile return.

An encounter between an innocent pilgrim and the modern world is one of Hesse's favorite literary devices. When Siddhartha meets Kamaswami, Siddhartha's innocence highlights the hypocrisy and spiritual poverty of his new world, which involves materialism and commerce, two aspects of modernity. During Siddhartha's initial job interview with Kamaswami, Siddhartha's answers to the questions are both honest and backhanded. When Kamaswami asks Siddhartha how he managed to live with so few possessions, Siddhartha says he has never really thought about what he lacked or how he should live. This response is a slap in Kamaswami's face, since Siddhartha is actually pointing out the poverty in Kamaswami's value system. Kamaswami initially intends to criticize Siddhartha by pointing out his lack of practical experience, but Siddhartha responds by calling into question the very criteria that determine whether some experiences are more practical than others. Siddhartha's lack of desire for material possessions is not the weakness Kamaswami might think. Instead, Siddhartha shows it as an asset in the business world. If one does not fear success or failure, one can act more aggressively.

Kamala is a master instructor of the truths of the material world, just as Gotama was a master instructor of the truths of the spiritual world. Kamala has an ability to find "stillness and sanctuary" within herself. She can steel herself against the outward flow of the world by retreating into this stillness. This ability is rare, and Siddhartha notices that the people immersed in the material world are trapped within it and cannot see beyond the small triumphs and tribulations of their lives. Similarly, Gotama can transcend the spiritual world he discusses. Just as Kamala can teach the truths of the world of love yet maintain enough distance from these truths to avoid being controlled by them, Gotama understands that the truths he communicates are not the entirety of knowledge. By contrast, the Brahmins and Samanas are able to see things only in terms of the spiritual knowledge they preach. Alternative approaches to knowledge threaten them, and they reject the alternatives without truly considering them. Just as Gotama is able to see past the words he speaks and to see the connection between moments in the world, Kamala is able to sense a unique spiritual dimension in the realm of love. In this way, Kamala, though not enlightened, is as important an instructor of knowledge for Siddhartha as Gotama was.

SUMMARY: SAMSARA

In Kamaswami's employ, Siddhartha becomes wealthy and enjoys Kamala's intimate company. He lives this way for many years, becoming more and more successful at business. At first, while business is all a game, he feels superior to those who pursue worldly pleasures and riches. Gradually, however, he, too, falls under the spell of possessions. He looks and acts like a wealthy merchant, wearing the finest clothes, eating rich food, entertaining dancers, and gambling, but he finds that the spiritual voice within him has died. Even his continued relationship with Kamala brings him little peace.

Some twenty years after his arrival, he notices that Kamala's face has wrinkles and his own hair has traces of gray. Siddhartha begins to have dreams that suggest the time may have come to move on. In one dream, he recalls a conversation with Kamala in which she expresses interest in Gotama, but Siddhartha dissuades her from seeking him out. In another dream, he finds the rare songbird Kamala keeps in a cage has died. He throws it out into the street, as though he discards all that is good and of value in his life. When he wakes up, he feels death in his heart. The inner voice that had prompted him to become a Samana, to turn away from the Buddha, and to face the unknown has been silent for a long time.

Distraught over these dreams, Siddhartha retreats to a pleasure garden to meditate. He considers his life in the city. The life he has made by apprenticing himself to Kamaswami seems only a diversion from his path to enlightenment. His nights of drinking, dancing, and eating have yielded a pleasant oblivion but have produced nothing. His relationship with Kamala has given him pleasure and taught him much about love, but it cannot continue forever if he aims to achieve enlightenment. He realizes that he has been playing at the game of *Samsara*, the cyclical path of normal life in which one lives, suffers, and dies. While it is important for him to have played this game, he does not need to keep playing it forever. He leaves the city in despair, without informing anyone of his departure. When Kamala learns of his disappearance, she frees her songbird from its golden cage. From this day on, Kamala accepts no more lovers, and she discovers she is pregnant with Siddhartha's child.

ANALYSIS: SAMSARA

Siddhartha has learned that asceticism is a dead end in his search for enlightenment, and he now learns that the same holds true for sensory indulgence—neither path, alone, leads to enlightenment, and the mastery of either asceticism or sensuality inevitably results in enslavement. Siddhartha has mastered almost everything he has attempted to do: He was a model son of the Brahmins and a skilled ascetic among the Samanas, and he is now mastering the art of love and desire. However, perfection leaves little room for variety or spontaneity, and Siddhartha discovers that he has become a slave to the very thing he has mastered, with no possible relief from the cycle of predictable events. Even his experiences with Kamala fit into this unending pattern. He is devoted to Kamala, but he is also bored. He must seek pleasure over and over again to keep boredom from returning, which leads only to more boredom. As the years accumulate, Siddhartha understands that the cycle of the senses revolves slowly but inevitably around the fixed point of death. Siddhartha had to immerse himself in the material world to learn all that it offered, but this sort of immersion ultimately traps most people, preventing them from ever achieving enlightenment. Siddhartha has to leave this world to escape the same fate.

Kamala rightly observes that Siddhartha initially sees the city with the eyes of a Samana, but Siddhartha's loss of spiritual detachment is inevitable. Siddhartha himself observes that his superior, distant feelings eventually disappear as he spends more time in the city. Such feelings can continue to exist only if he can maintain his distance from the material world and act as an impartial observer, but the more Siddhartha masters the material world, the more he becomes a part of it. He becomes almost equal to Kamaswami in business, and he becomes the greatest lover Kamala has ever had. In both cases, he becomes as good as his teachers, effectively becoming just like his teachers, which anchors him in the material world. He is no longer a thin, naked Samana but a wealthy, well-clothed, and well-fed merchant. The only aspects of his spiritual roots that remain are those isolated within his mind. As he gains material power, his spiritual power declines, until Siddhartha can no longer hear his inner voice. His spiritual roots are now a memory. Love and the material world have dragged Siddhartha away from the spiritual enlightenment he seeks.

Siddhartha's dream about the dead songbird suggests what could happen if Siddhartha continues on his current path, and it helps Siddhartha decide to leave the city. Kamala's actual release of the songbird upon Siddhartha's departure suggests that Siddhartha has experienced an awakening. When Siddhartha disappears, Kamaswami searches for him, thinking bandits have captured him, but Kamala shows no surprise—she has expected Siddhartha to leave. She releases the songbird as soon as she hears the news, clearly linking Siddhartha and the bird. The bird dies in Siddhartha's dream, and its death brings Siddhartha a feeling of complete spiritual emptiness. In the real world, the bird is freed, which suggests that Siddhartha has avoided the spiritual death foretold in the dream and has awakened from his slumber in the material world. Kamala is also on the verge of an awakening: after she releases the bird, she decides to take no more lovers. She changes her life in the wake of Siddhartha's departure, and her pregnancy indicates a radical change that parallels the change Siddhartha will undergo next.

SUMMARY: BY THE RIVER
Siddhartha leaves the city and wanders back into the countryside, feeling miserable and contemplating suicide. He ponders the paths he has taken in search of enlightenment. With the Samanas, he abstained from all physical indulgence, and in the city he satiated

every physical desire, but neither of these approaches brought him closer to enlightenment. Siddhartha wanders aimlessly back to the river he had crossed with the ferryman. As he is about to let himself slip into the water and end his useless life, the sacred word Om reverberates within him, and his slumbering spirit awakens. He recognizes the folly of his contemplated suicide, lies down in the grass, and falls asleep.

Siddhartha wakes up to find that a meditating Buddhist monk has joined him. He realizes it is Govinda, but Govinda does not recognize him. Siddhartha introduces himself, and Govinda tells him that he is still a follower of Gotama. Govinda remains convinced that his role as a spiritual pilgrim is still correct. Siddhartha replies that he too is a spiritual pilgrim, but his old friend is skeptical. After all, Govinda points out, Siddhartha is well fed and looks like a rich merchant. Siddhartha tells Govinda an abbreviated version of what has happened in his life since they parted, and repeats that he too is still a pilgrim in search of enlightenment. Govinda remains skeptical, but he bows respectfully to Siddhartha and goes on his way.

Siddhartha feels he can learn nothing more by joining again with the Samanas or the followers of Gotama. Eventually, Siddhartha reasons that his overthinking compromised his previous attempts at enlightenment. His zealous attempts to attach himself to religious movements or ways of being that appeared to offer enlightenment have been in error. He has, in a sense, been trying too hard to find what he seeks. Siddhartha stares down into the river and begins to feel a strong affection for it. He resolves to not leave its side.

ANALYSIS: BY THE RIVER

When Siddhartha encounters the river, he realizes that the past is essential to life but does not determine the future. This certainty prepares him to move forward with his search for enlightenment. At the river, Siddhartha falls asleep, and when he wakes up, he knows he is a new man—he has been reborn. This rebirth differs from that of "Awakening," when Siddhartha tried to consciously deny the past to make way for the future. The present rebirth confronts the past more directly and relates it to life in the present. The past reveals itself through memory and exists now as a bridge between the past and the future. Siddhartha sees his mistake in trying to control the direction of his life, for he could do this only by submission to the repetitive cycle of time. He considers that a long lifetime of experience and wandering has brought him nowhere at all. However, the river now grants him self-knowledge and sets him on a new course. Siddhartha has learned the Buddhist lesson of "right conduct": he must take the way that comes naturally, heeding only his own voice, without trying to arrange the course of discovery in advance.

The appearance of Om signals the return of Siddhartha's spiritual self and the beginning of the final path that will lead him to enlightenment. Om conveys the very essence of life, and each time it appears in *Siddhartha* it brings Siddhartha back in touch with his pure and primal self. When Siddhartha rejects his suicidal impulse, Om awakens him to a higher self, reminding him of the knowledge and divinity he has experienced throughout his search. The knowledge learned reappears because it is essential to what is to come. On the first page of *Siddhartha*, Om appears as a central, foundational teaching of the Brahmins. In this appearance it saves Siddhartha's life and leads to awakening. It will reappear in the voice of the river as Siddhartha finally succeeds in attaining an enlightened state. Siddhartha's deep sleep and his awakening after hearing Om bring understanding. Now, having failed to reach enlightenment through the extremes of self-denial and self-gratification, Siddhartha prepares to find a balance between the two.

Govinda cannot recognize Siddhartha when he encounters Siddhartha by the river, nor can Govinda recognize the truth about his own search for enlightenment. Govinda stays true to the Buddhist path even though he has not achieved the wisdom he seeks, and he cannot see that the path has failed him. Siddhartha, on the other hand, is able to glean truths from the Brahmin, Samana, and Buddhist worlds, but he is also able to recognize that none of these traditions will give him the enlightenment he seeks. Siddhartha, unlike Govinda, can see the flaws in potential paths to enlightenment, and he has the courage to abandon failed paths for other, more promising options. Though Govinda eventually does reach enlightenment, he does so only because Siddhartha, with his superior spiritual powers, is there to help him. Hesse doesn't make clear whether the enlightenment Siddhartha transmits to Govinda is temporary or lasting. If Siddhartha gives Govinda only a fleeting glimpse of it, chances are good that Govinda will continue to search for his own enlightenment.

SUMMARY: THE FERRYMAN
Having resolved to live a new life by the river, Siddhartha soon meets the ferryman, the same one who had helped Siddhartha cross the river years before. The ferryman, named Vasudeva, remembers

Siddhartha as the Samana who had slept in his hut years ago, and he invites Siddhartha to share it once more. Siddhartha says that though he looks like a merchant, he wants to live with Vasudeva beside the river. When Siddhartha tells Vasudeva his story, Vasudeva knows the river has spoken to Siddhartha and grants his request to be his assistant.

Siddhartha works, eats, and sleeps alongside Vasudeva, while Vasudeva instructs Siddhartha in the practical aspects of being a ferryman. During this period, Siddhartha gently plies Vasudeva about the connection between his seeming enlightened detachment and his life at the river. Vasudeva replies that the river has many secrets to tell and lessons to offer, and that he will help Siddhartha learn these secrets and lessons. The first lesson Siddhartha learns from the river is that time does not exist. When he asks Vasudeva if he has learned this secret as well, Vasudeva smiles broadly and says yes. Siddhartha is excited with the discovery and realizes that all suffering, self-torment, anxieties, difficulties, and hostilities are anchored in time, and all will disappear when people overcome the idea of time. Some time later Vasudeva smiles even more broadly when Siddhartha notices that the river has many voices, that it sounds like all things and all people, and that when the voices are all heard in unison the sound Om appears.

News that the Buddha is dying sweeps through the land, and pilgrims by the hundreds begin flocking to pay him homage. Among them are Kamala and her son, an unwilling traveler who longs for the comforts of his home. A short distance from the river, she stops to rest, and a poisonous snake bites her. Vasudeva hears the son's cry for help, carries Kamala to the ferry, and brings her across the river to their hut. Siddhartha immediately recognizes her, and he thinks her son looks familiar. Then he realizes that the boy must be his son. Kamala lives long enough to speak to Siddhartha. In this last conversation, she knows she need not see the Buddha to fulfill her wish of seeing an enlightened one—Siddhartha is no different from the Buddha. Siddhartha himself feels blessed, for now he has a son.

ANALYSIS: THE FERRYMAN

Siddhartha has spent many years pursuing enlightenment, and his experiences have shown him that enlightenment can't be taught. However, in Vasudeva, Siddhartha finds the ideal teacher—in a sense, a teacher who does not teach. Vasudeva himself admits he is not a teacher: "If I could talk and teach, I would perhaps be a teacher, but as it is I am only a ferryman," he says. Vasudeva listens to Siddhartha and encourages him to listen to the river. Siddhartha surrenders to Vasudeva his entire self, even his clothes, in order to follow his example in leading a life of calm fulfillment and wisdom. Vasudeva gives Siddhartha food and shelter, but he does not impose on him his own wisdom and experiences. Siddhartha follows Vasudeva's example but reaches enlightenment on his own. Vasudeva is a guide, both literally and figuratively. While he guides Siddhartha back and forth across the river, he also affirms Siddhartha's spiritual progress and encourages him to continue searching. Vasudeva is poised between the ordinary world and the world of enlightenment. He acts as an intermediary for seekers such as Siddhartha, who venture to the river and hope to pass from one world to the other.

One of the most important lessons the river teaches Siddhartha is that time does not exist, and that the present is all that matters. Siddhartha can now see that all life is unified, just as the river is in all places at one time. By evoking the symbol of the river to suggest the unity of life, Hesse refers to the philosophy and religion of Taoism, which maintains that a force, called *Tao*, flows through and connects all living things and the universe, and that balancing the Tao results in complete happiness. The primary symbol of Taoism is the Yin Yang, a circular shape with one black section and one white section fitting perfectly together.

The Yin Yang suggests the balance of opposites, an idea that the final portion of *Siddhartha* explores. The river, with its constant movement and presence, reveals the existence of opposites such as flux and permanence and time and timelessness. Siddhartha has attempted to find enlightenment in many different ways, but only when he accepts that opposites can co-exist does he reach enlightenment.

The river can be all places at once, and its essence never changes. In this way Siddhartha resembles the river. Despite the changing aspects of his experience, his essential self has always remained the same. He actually calls his life a river and uses this comparison to determine that time does not exist. Siddhartha, with the help of the river and Vasudeva, is finally able to learn the last elements necessary to achieve enlightenment. Vasudeva reveals the true importance of the river to Siddhartha: the river can teach Siddhartha everything he needs to know, beginning with how to listen. This doctrine suggests that knowledge resides in the present time and place, and that Siddhartha, from his position in the here and now, can discover all there is to know. Siddhartha understands that time does not really exist, since everything can be learned from the present moment. Without a fear of time, worry about the fleetingness of life, or the weight of boredom, Siddhartha can achieve enlightenment.

SUMMARY: THE SON

After Kamala's funeral, Siddhartha does his best to console and provide for his son, but the boy is spoiled and cynical. Siddhartha's son dislikes life with the two ferrymen, wishing to return to the city and the life of wealth he knows. Siddhartha cannot convince him that fine clothes, a soft bed, and servants have little meaning. Siddhartha believes he should raise his son himself, and Vasudeva at first agrees. Though he tries as hard as he can to make his son happy and to show him how to live a good life, Siddhartha finds his son filled with rage. His son steals from Vasudeva and Siddhartha and berates them, making their lives unpleasant. Siddhartha finds that, though he has never been able to love before, he now loves his son, and as a result he dismisses his son's behavior as the inevitable result of Kamala's death. He believes that in time his son will come to follow the same path he and Vasudeva have followed.

Vasudeva, however, eventually tells Siddhartha that the son should be allowed to leave if he wants to. Even though old men may be fully satisfied ferrying people across a river, a young boy may be unhappy in such conditions, he says. Vasudeva also reminds Siddhartha that his own father had not been able to prevent him from joining the Samanas or from learning the lessons of worldliness in the city. The boy should follow his own path, even if that makes Siddhartha unhappy. Siddhartha disagrees, feeling that the bond between father and son is important and, as his own flesh and blood, his son will likewise be driven to search for enlightenment. The river, where true enlightenment and learning can be found, should be an ideal spot for the boy to spend his days.

One night the son yells that Siddhartha has neither the authority nor the will to discipline him. The son screams that a ferryman living by a river is the last thing he would ever want to become, that he would rather be a murderer than a man like Siddhartha. Siddhartha has no reply. The next morning, Siddhartha discovers that his son has run away, stealing all of Siddhartha's and Vasudeva's money. Vasudeva believes that Siddhartha should let the son go, but Siddhartha feels he must follow his son, if only out of concern for his safety. Siddhartha gives chase but soon realizes his task is futile. He knows his son will hide if he sees Siddhartha. Still, Siddhartha keeps going until he has reached the city.

As he looks at the city, memories of his life there come rushing back. He remembers the time he spent with Kamaswami and, especially, with Kamala. In a flash, Siddhartha acknowledges he must let his son go. He understands that no amount of reasoning will convince him to stay. Although the son may grow into a spiritual pilgrim like Siddhartha, the quest must be undertaken on his own. Siddhartha falls to the ground, exhausted, and is awakened by Vasudeva, who has secretly followed him. Together, they return to the river.

ANALYSIS: THE SON

Through his interactions with his son, Siddhartha learns the Buddhist lesson of "right endeavor," and that it is not possible to impose one's knowledge of the timeless upon one who is still subject to the limits of time. Siddhartha does not realize he is trying to make his son in his own image, but his son realizes it and resents Siddhartha for doing so. Siddhartha is, after all, little more than a stranger to the son. Even though Vasudeva reminds Siddhartha that no one can determine the boy's calling, Siddhartha is blinded by love, and he ignores something he already knows: Everyone must follow his own voice to enlightenment. He has learned for himself that no one can teach enlightenment, and that enlightenment must be found within. Siddhartha tries to prescribe his son's life just as his father had once tried to prescribe his, and he attempts to impose his views on his son. Siddhartha has come full circle. Just as he ran away from his own father, his son runs away in search of his own path.

Although Siddhartha's road to enlightenment led him through the material world of Kama, he has tested himself only against materialism, not against love—and the appearance of his son forces him to undertake this challenge. Although Siddhartha has attained peace as a ferryman, he is fallible because he has not confronted love itself. Many compelling reasons exist for Siddhartha to allow his son to return to the city, but, blinded by love, he forgets that enlightenment must come from within and tries to impose his views on his son. Since leaving the followers of Gotama, Siddhartha has maintained that a journey toward peace and enlightenment must come from within, and Vasudeva points out Siddhartha's contradiction of his own beliefs. Logically, Siddhartha should recognize his error in this situation. The fact that Siddhartha ignores his most fundamental belief is a testament to how much he loves his son.

> *He remembered how once, as a youth, he had*
> *compelled his father to let him go and join the ascetic,*
> *how he had taken leave of him, how he had gone and*
> *never returned. Had not his father also suffered the*
> *same pain that he was now suffering for his son?*
> (See QUOTATIONS, p. 51)

SUMMARY: OM

Siddhartha meditates for many days on the loss of his son. His pain and sadness are great. One day, Siddhartha looks into the river, and as the water laughs at him for letting the wound burn so deeply, he realizes that life has an inevitable flow, just like a river. When Siddhartha was a boy, he left his own father despite great protestations. Now his own son has left him. Because of this doubled perspective, Siddhartha sympathizes with his father and his son at the same time. He understands that some sorrows in life cannot be prevented and will pass from generation to generation throughout time. Siddhartha feels a new sense of peace. That night he tells Vasudeva all he has felt, and Vasudeva seems to absorb all of his sorrows. Siddhartha realizes that Vasudeva is as enlightened as the Buddha, and that he seems like a god.

The old ferryman invites him to listen more closely to the river. As they sit on the bank, all the images of his life dance before him. He hears voices of joy and sorrow, good and evil, laughter and mourning. But he does not let himself be caught up by any single voice and hears only the single word Om. Sitting beside Vasudeva at the river, Siddhartha realizes that his Self is a part of the great perfection that is all of the voices in the world speaking together. Siddhartha no longer doubts his place in the world or second-guesses his actions. His face now reflects the same divine understanding that he first noticed on Vasudeva's face when he met him. In this hour Siddhartha stops battling his fate, and his eyes glow with the serenity of knowledge. When Vasudeva sees this, he says that he has been waiting for this moment, and he departs to the forest, leaving Siddhartha as the ferryman.

ANALYSIS: OM

In order to achieve enlightenment, Siddhartha must give up what he loves. Siddhartha's difficulty with giving up his son suggests that love is the toughest challenge Siddhartha has faced during his quest and that Siddhartha is actually no different than anyone who has experienced love. Losing his son is difficult for Siddhartha, but what he experiences now as a father is the same as what he experienced years before as a son. When he sees a reflection of himself in the river, a reflection of his father is superimposed upon it, as though his father is subject to the same trial Siddhartha is presently undergoing. He sees a vision of the self in both past and future. His son acts in the way he himself had acted, and he will follow a path of his own choosing in the same way Siddhartha did. Similarly, Siddhartha is acting just as his father did so many years ago, trying to keep his son at home, despite his own wisdom. These similarities, which persist despite all that Siddhartha has learned, suggest that the present moment truly does contain all of time. The present moment contains a concentration of experiences that would take several lifetimes to undergo. Siddhartha knows not only that he himself is always the same despite the changes in his life but also that he is the same as all others in the world.

In "Om," suffering acts as a humanizing force for Siddhartha. Through suffering, Siddhartha finds unity among his roles as father, traveler, and son, as well as unity between the past and future. In the past, Siddhartha has looked scornfully at people in the mortal world, but at this moment his suffering allows him to see his unity with the world. He no longer stands above and is no better than anyone else. His suffering has shown him that he is like them, and only in realizing his similarities with the rest of the world can he achieve the compassion necessary for true enlightenment. Vasudeva and Siddhartha have both experienced human suffering, and just as Vasudeva returns to the divine, so too will Siddhartha one day. Both have overcome their suffering in order to achieve enlightenment.

Vasudeva's profession as a ferryman, one who guides a person from one side of the river to the other, fits well with his status as spiritual guide. If one side of the river represents enlightenment, and the other side represents the life as it was lived before enlightenment, then Vasudeva helps to convey people to their final destination. However, people must first reach the river of their own accord and know that they seek to reach the other bank. He does not tell people where they must go but helps those who are ready to complete the journey. When Siddhartha achieves enlightenment, Vasudeva leaves him, and Siddhartha inherits the position Vasudeva previously held. In this way, a level of equality is demonstrated between Vasudeva and Siddhartha. Although Vasudeva is often described in divine terms, he does not maintain the power relationship that would typically exist between student and teacher, or between the divine and the mortal. When he departs, Siddhartha is his equal. He has guided Siddhartha to his final destination and can now depart, unlike a teacher who would have to stay behind to continue teaching others.

> *No longer knowing whether time existed, whether this display had lasted a second or a hundred years, whether there was a Siddhartha, or a Gotama, a Self and others, wounded deeply by a divine arrow which gave him pleasure, deeply enchanted and exalted, Govinda stood yet a while bending over Siddhartha's peaceful face which he had just kissed, which had just been the stage of all present and future forms.*
>
> *(See* QUOTATIONS*, p. 52)*

SUMMARY: GOVINDA

Govinda returns to the river to seek enlightenment. He has heard of a wise man living there, but when he arrives, he does not recognize Siddhartha. When Govinda asks him for advice, Siddhartha tells him with a smile that he is searching too hard and that he is possessed by his goal, and then calls him by name. Govinda is as amazed now as when he failed to recognize Siddhartha at the river years earlier. Govinda still follows Gotama but has not attained the kind of enlightenment that Siddhartha now radiates. So he asks Siddhartha to teach him what he knows.

Govinda stays the night in Siddhartha's hut, and Siddhartha gives advice that is a summary of his wisdom. He warns Govinda, however, that his wisdom can't be taught, and that no one can teach the wisdom because verbal explanations are limited and can never communicate the entirety of enlightenment. Knowledge can be passed along, but individuals must earn their own wisdom. Siddhartha points out that when one attempts to teach, as the Buddha did, then one must divide or categorize the world into Samsara and Nirvana, into disappointment and truth, into sorrow and salvation. Siddhartha has learned that for every truth, there is an opposite truth. No one is ever fully saintly or fully sinful, and if someone appears to be so, it is merely a deception that time is real. The world is never incomplete or on its path to completeness. It is complete at every moment. Grace carries every sin, all babies carry death, and all the dying carry eternal life. Siddhartha says he wants only to love the world as it has been, as it is, and as it will be, and to consider all creatures with love, admiration, and reverence.

Govinda asks Siddhartha if there is not some additional advice that might help him. Govinda points out that he is very old and has little time to reach the final understanding Siddhartha has attained. Siddhartha tells Govinda to kiss him on the forehead. When he does, Govinda sees the timeless flow of forces and images pass before his eyes, just as Siddhartha had envisioned them in the flowing river. With tears streaming from his eyes, Govinda bows down to Siddhartha, whose smiling face is no different from that of the enlightened Buddha. Govinda and Siddhartha have both finally achieved the enlightenment they set out to find in the days of their youth.

ANALYSIS: GOVINDA

This chapter represents the Buddhist idea of "right rapture," with an enlightened one who rejoices in his enlightenment yet mocks the glory of his knowledge by admitting that full communication is impossible. Yet though Siddhartha cannot fully explain his enlightenment to Govinda, his face is still a vision of truth for Govinda. The face of an enlightened person, whether Gotama, Vasudeva, or Siddhartha, is similarly illuminated. When he looks at Siddhartha, Govinda sees thousands of faces, and though these faces change continuously, they are still Siddhartha's face. While Govinda looks at this face, he realizes, as Kamala did, that it appears no different from Gotama's. Thus the goal Siddhartha has realized for himself, the destruction of time, is visible for Govinda in the face of an enlightened person. Govinda, who has searched for enlightenment without full knowledge of the implications of his search, has struck upon wisdom. No difference exists now between seeker and sage, no difference exists between Siddhartha and Gotama, and no disunity is possible for the enlightened one who has found his way to the wisdom of the other shore.

The mentoring relationships between Vasudeva and Siddhartha and between Siddhartha and Govinda suggest that even though no one can teach the way to enlightenment, seekers still can be guided. At the end of *Siddhartha*, Siddhartha presumably will carry on as the ferryman now that Vasudeva has left. Siddhartha's son bears Siddhartha's name, implying that he may ultimately follow in Siddhartha's footsteps. As ferryman, Siddhartha will pass back and forth between the two worlds that the river symbolically divides and unites, which suggests that the polarities of life will always exist.

Like Vasudeva, Siddhartha will be of service to those who cross over the water and will give his passengers the opportunity to listen to the river's message, though few will hear it. Siddhartha will guide those who need guidance, but he will not force his wisdom on those who do not wish to hear it. Govinda comes to Siddhartha in search of a concrete explanation of how to achieve enlightenment, and when Siddhartha's words fail, as any instruction must, Siddhartha is able to communicate his knowledge wordlessly, through a kiss. Siddhartha guides Govinda into understanding all the knowledge Siddhartha has. In this way, Govinda achieves the enlightenment he would never have achieved had Siddhartha attempted to teach him instead of guide him.

Siddhartha's attempt to explain enlightenment points out a fundamental difference in how various groups and teachers perceive Nirvana. Siddhartha says that while teachers such as Gotama and the Samanas insist that Nirvana is a state that can be obtained *one day*, Nirvana is actually going on all around us. All men can be sinners, and all can be saints, but regardless, all things contain the potential for Nirvana and perfection. A sinner may be on the path to becoming a saint. A gambler may evolve to one day into a Buddha. Therefore, all people are sacred. Siddhartha also implies that a sacredness exists in all things. When he shows Govinda a stone, he wants to convey that even the most humble object is sacred, since that stone may one day turn into soil, which may become a plant, an animal, a man, or even a Buddha. Therefore, Siddhartha reasons, everything is sacred and contains wondrous potential. Enlightenment, rather than being a state one finally reaches, is instead a state already obtained even as it is sought.

IMPORTANT QUOTATIONS EXPLAINED

1.   "Siddhartha," he said, "why are you waiting?"
     "You know why."
     "Will you go on standing and waiting until it is day,
noon, evening?"
     "I will stand and wait."
     "You will grow tired, Siddhartha."
     "I will grow tired."
     "You will fall asleep, Siddhartha."
     "I will not fall asleep."
     "You will die, Siddhartha."
     "I will die."

In this section from the opening chapter "The Brahmin's Son," Siddhartha engages in a loaded dialogue with his father. Siddhartha is a spiritual pilgrim, and though it is clear he earnestly desires to seek truth and transcendent knowledge, Hesse does not yet reveal the full extent of his convictions. Siddhartha has met the wandering Samanas, and he is entranced by the possibilities of adopting the Samanas' ascetic lifestyle. In this dialogue with his father, Siddhartha makes clear for the first time just how solid his convictions are and how deeply he feels he must search for spiritual fulfillment. Siddhartha's father strongly disagrees with Siddhartha's decision to join the Samanas, since Siddhartha will be leaving not only his family but also his religion. Leaving his religion is an additional slap in Siddhartha's father's face, because Siddhartha's father is in effect a religious leader. Here, Siddhartha confronts his father with total conviction. This conviction will appear again later, when Siddhartha's own son decides to leave his life as a ferryman and return to the city of his birth.

2.   Siddhartha learned a great deal from the Samanas; he
      learned many ways of losing the Self. He traveled along the
      path of self-denial through pain, through voluntary
      suffering and conquering of pain, through hunger, thirst and
      fatigue. He traveled the way of self-denial through
      meditation, through the emptying of the mind through all
      images. Along these and other paths did he learn to travel.
      He lost his Self a thousand times and for days on end he
      dwelt in non-being. But although the paths took him away
      from Self, in the end they always led back to it.

This passage from the second chapter, "With the Samanas,"
describes Siddhartha's initial attempt to find enlightenment, and his
ultimate frustration with it. The Samanas advocate eliminating the
Self in order to achieve spiritual fulfillment. They believe that when
personal feelings and needs are eliminated, whatever remains will be
transcendent. The Samanas believe that one can effectively eliminate the Self by denying the senses. Siddhartha and Govinda give
themselves over completely to this technique, but as this passage
makes clear, Siddhartha does not succeed. While he can lose himself
temporarily in his efforts to resist hunger, thirst, and fatigue, Siddhartha always comes back to his Self. The exercises of the Samanas
offer progress, but the progress is only temporary.

   This passage reveals a crucial element of Siddhartha's approach
to seeking enlightenment. Siddhartha, though he is a dedicated spiritual pilgrim, does not like the wait-and-see approach. When a
method of spiritual pursuit loses its efficacy or exhibits limitations,
Siddhartha moves on to another. Siddhartha makes some spiritual
progress with the Samanas, and he is certainly better off with them
than he was in his home village. However, even the oldest Samanas
have not yet attained Nirvana, and Siddhartha will not wait around.
He is trapped in a cycle of losing and regaining his Self, and he
believes there must be a better way to Nirvana.

QUOTATIONS

3.   "[T]here is one thing that this clear, worthy instruction does
not contain; it does not contain the secret of what the
Illustrious One himself experienced—he alone among
hundreds of thousands. That is what I thought and realized
when I heard your teachings. That is why I am going on my
way—not to seek another doctrine, for I know there is none,
but to leave all doctrines and all teachers and to reach my
goal alone—or die."

This excerpt, from the chapter "Gotama," is part of Siddhartha's
parting dialogue with Gotama the Buddha. Here, Siddhartha further refines and revises the principles that will guide his spiritual
quest. He clearly defines the problem he sees in Gotama's teaching:
Gotama has achieved enlightenment himself, but his achievement
does not guarantee that he is able to enlighten others. This doubt
serves as a centerpiece to Siddhartha's argument. Siddhartha points
out that Gotama did not have a teacher to show him how to attain
Nirvana. Siddhartha finally proves that following the commands of
an enlightened man does not necessarily lead to becoming enlightened oneself. Siddhartha goes no further. He does not dislike Gotama, and, in fact, he praises Gotama's teachings and concedes that
attaining Nirvana certainly qualifies one to teach others about the
world. Siddhartha maintains only that attaining Nirvana does not
appear to enable one to teach others to reach it.

Siddhartha's problems with Gotama's teaching helps Siddhartha
shape his own quest for enlightenment into a self-directed one. When
Siddhartha goes straight from his many years of asceticism to a life of
indulgence and sensual gratification with Kamala, the contrast may at
first seem jarring or implausibly radical. However, passages such as the
one above do account for Siddhartha's extreme transition. He has
resolved to apprentice himself to no other person in his quest for Nirvana. While Kamala teaches him to enjoy physical love, and Vasudeva
teaches him to listen to the river, Siddhartha's journey remains self-
directed for the remainder of the novel. All notions of where Nirvana
might be found now come from within.

4.   His face resembled that of another person, whom he had once known and loved and even feared. It resembled the face of his father, the Brahmin. He remembered how once, as a youth, he had compelled his father to let him go and join the ascetic, how he had taken leave of him, how he had gone and never returned. Had not his father also suffered the same pain that he was now suffering for his son?

This quotation appears in the chapter titled "Om." After Siddhartha's son leaves, Siddhartha resumes the life of a ferryman with Vasudeva. Siddhartha has been sick at heart about his son's decision to flee back to the city, and the passage of time has not helped to ease the pain. Here, Siddhartha looks into the river, and he sees his father in his reflection in the water. He remembers his own departure from home in the midst of unhappy circumstances, and he remembers that his departure hurt his father, just as his son's departure hurt Siddhartha himself. He realizes that he could not have stopped his son from leaving, just as Siddhartha's own father could not have stopped Siddhartha. Although Siddhartha wanted to share with his son all he had learned about life, he accepts now that his son will have to come into his own understanding. Siddhartha could not have helped him in his search for meaning any more than Siddhartha's own father was able to help Siddhartha. These observations and the solace Siddhartha draws from them mark the beginning of his understanding of life as a river, which is one of the most important aspects of the Nirvana he eventually attains. Like the flow of the river, events in Siddhartha's life seem inevitable, repetitive, and even circular. Trying to resist the river's current is senseless. For the first time, Siddhartha truly internalizes these notions, and he begins to understand the ideas of timelessness and peace.

5.   No longer knowing whether time existed, whether this display had lasted a second or a hundred years, whether there was a Siddhartha, or a Gotama, a Self and others, wounded deeply by a divine arrow which gave him pleasure, deeply enchanted and exalted, Govinda stood yet a while bending over Siddhartha's peaceful face which he had just kissed, which had just been the stage of all present and future forms. His countenance was unchanged after the mirror of the thousand-fold forms had disappeared from the surface. He smiled peacefully and gently, perhaps very graciously, perhaps very mockingly, exactly as the Illustrious One had smiled.

This quotation appears near the end of "Govinda," the novel's final chapter, and it serves as both Siddhartha's ultimate vindication and a contradiction to Siddhartha's beliefs. First, it leaves no question as to whether Siddhartha has succeeded in his lifelong quest to reach enlightenment. Siddhartha's face is the same touchstone of enlightenment once known only to Gotama, and Govinda can actually taste the Nirvana he emanates. Govinda finally acknowledges that Siddhartha's methods were the right ones all along. While Govinda's road toward Nirvana was more traditionally pious, Siddhartha's path proved more successful. All along Siddhartha had claimed Nirvana can come only from within, and that teachers could not impart enlightenment to students. Govinda seems to accept this contention at last.

However, an ambiguity emerges as this chapter draws to a close. Govinda seems to have achieved Nirvana by kissing Siddhartha's forehead. This description of Govinda's transcendent understanding is remarkably similar to Siddhartha's own experience of Nirvana. If Siddhartha can transmit Nirvana through a kiss, however, he contradicts his own central belief that Nirvana can come only from within. Possibly, Siddhartha gives Govinda merely a glimpse of true enlightenment, not enlightenment itself, essentially pointing the way for Govinda, much as Vasudeva pointed the way for him.

KEY FACTS

FULL TITLE
Siddhartha

AUTHOR
Hermann Hesse

TYPE OF WORK
Novel

GENRE
Spiritual and Religious Novel

LANGUAGE
German

TIME AND PLACE WRITTEN
1919–1921, Switzerland

DATE OF FIRST PUBLICATION
1922

PUBLISHER
Bantam

NARRATOR
An unnamed narrator tracks Siddhartha's spiritual progress.

POINT OF VIEW
Third-person omniscient. The point of view follows Siddhartha most closely.

TONE
Measured without being detached; formal

TENSE
Past

SETTING (TIME)
Concurrent with the life of Buddha, estimated at around 625 B.C.

SETTING (PLACE)
India

PROTAGONIST
Siddhartha

MAJOR CONFLICT
Siddhartha searches for total spiritual enlightenment.

RISING ACTION
Siddhartha experiments with different teachers and approaches
to Nirvana, and when they prove unsatisfactory, he turns his
search inward.

CLIMAX
Siddhartha finally achieves total spiritual understanding as he
sits beside Vasudeva and listens to the river.

FALLING ACTION
Siddhartha meets Govinda and shares the Nirvana he has
attained.

THEMES
The search for spiritual enlightenment; inner vs. exterior
guidance; the wisdom of indirection

MOTIFS
Love; Om; polarities

SYMBOLS
The river; the ferryman; the smile

FORESHADOWING
Siddhartha's sloughing-off of his father's traditional Brahmin
beliefs foreshadows Siddhartha's future loss of his own son.
Siddhartha's observation to Govinda that not even the eldest of
the Samanas has attained Nirvana, and Govinda's subsequent
dismissal of the statement, foreshadows Govinda's inability to
find Nirvana by following the teachings of others.
The first appearance of the peaceful ferryman, whom Siddhartha
encounters on his way to the city, foreshadows Siddhartha's own
future as a ferryman and as a man of total spiritual peace.

Study Questions and Essay Topics

Study Questions

1. SIDDHARTHA *features substantial activity and narrative action. At the same time, it is about one man's largely internal spiritual quest. What is the relationship between the internal and exterior worlds of* SIDDHARTHA? *How does Siddhartha negotiate these worlds?*

Siddhartha is driven to extremes by his desire for spiritual enlightenment and understanding. While he embraces the extremes of physicality in this novel, the initial spark of desire comes from within him. Siddhartha's initial project is to negate the Self. The Samanas, and to some extent Gotama the Buddha, preach this negation as the catalyst for enlightenment. They claim that one can negate the Self through the mollification of the senses and the elimination of desire. While desire can be mental and physical, the senses are decidedly rooted in physicality. When people describe Siddhartha as looking "like a Samana," the effects of this sensual negation are what they see.

Siddhartha pursues the opposite sensual extreme during his life with Kamala. He enjoys sex with Kamala, as well as food, dancing, and drinking. Siddhartha does not attempt to find a balance between this new world and the ascetic world he left behind. Though sex and drinking are new to him, he does not attempt to negotiate a level of comfort or moderation. His goal is to attain Nirvana through excess. However, excess, like fasting, fails to provide the desired effect. When Siddhartha eventually does attain Nirvana, he does not do so through a sensual extreme. Rather, he has learned to find a balance in his life by the river. His physicality reflects his sense of peace, but he does not radiate the effects of a physical extreme. Instead, he exudes the peace he initially noticed in Vasudeva's eyes many years ago.

2.   *Discuss the ways Siddhartha attempts to attain spiritual enlightenment. Which approaches are successful? Which ones are not successful, and which ones have limited effectiveness? How does Siddhartha progress from one approach to the other?*

When Siddhartha leaves his boyhood village, he is armed only with the desire to understand himself and reach enlightenment. He has no concrete, long-term plan for himself other than to seek spiritual fulfillment, and he follows many different paths to reach his goal. Siddhartha employs a kind of process of elimination as he tries one tactic after another. Although his journey is a spiritual one, in many cases Siddhartha uses an almost mathematical calculation to decide how to proceed. When he decides to move from one way of life to another, his choice is always decidedly analytical.

Siddhartha initially leaves his father the Brahmin for a life among the Samanas. Although his father is a religious leader, Nirvana has never been his stated goal. The Samanas, in contrast, explicitly seek the spiritually transcendent. Soon, Gotama the Buddha tempts Siddhartha to leave the Samanas because Gotama has attained Nirvana. Siddhartha reasons that the Samanas cannot be as effective as Gotama if they have never found enlightenment. Siddhartha eventually leaves Gotama as well. He concludes that although Gotama has attained Nirvana, his teachings will not necessarily lead others to it. Siddhartha's subsequent indulgences in the city may seem haphazard, but they are prompted by a meticulous application of the process of elimination. Siddhartha does not want to deny himself any physical experience. When he lies in the pleasure garden and resolves to leave the city, he is prompted to do so by his dream of Kamala's bird. This dream allows him to understand the emptiness of city life. When Siddhartha begins to live alongside Vasudeva, he realizes that Nirvana cannot be taught. Rather, Siddhartha intends to follow in the steps of the ferryman and learn to read the river for himself.

3. *Consider Siddhartha's relationship with Govinda. How are they similar, and how are they different? What are the narrative functions of Govinda's reappearance throughout the novel? How does their relationship impact the novel's ending?*

Govinda is Siddhartha's childhood friend and becomes his partner as a spiritual pilgrim. He serves a variety of functions in the novel, both to further the plot and to reveal aspects of Siddhartha we might not otherwise see. Govinda often provides a sounding board for Siddhartha's ideas. The dialogue between the two friends allows Hesse to show instead of simply tell what Siddhartha is thinking. Govinda often disagrees with Siddhartha, which allows Siddhartha to expound specifically on why he believes he must act. Govinda differs with Siddhartha on the efficacy of the spiritual approach offered by the Samanas, and almost does not accompany Siddhartha when he leaves. Likewise, Siddhartha remains skeptical about Gotama's approach, but Govinda holds fast to his beliefs. When Siddhartha ultimately leaves Gotama's camp, Govinda's decision to stay helps to cushion the indictment of the Buddha.

Govinda's reappearance after he and Siddhartha initially part ways highlights how different Siddhartha is now from the man he could have remained had he stayed with Govinda. Govinda functions almost as an alternate-reality version of Siddhartha. Govinda stays true to the teachings of Gotama, a path Siddhartha might well have followed himself. Thus, the first contrast between the two friends is a physical one. Siddhartha changes, while Govinda remains an ascetic. However, Siddhartha ultimately succeeds in attaining Nirvana while Govinda does not. The final meeting of the two friends drives home this point. Siddhartha is able to give Govinda a glimpse of his enlightenment. The friends' high regard for one another lasts throughout the novel, and both men are respectful of the choices the other has made. This respect persists even as Siddhartha is undeniably acknowledged as the more successful of the two.

Suggested Essay Topics

1. *Discuss the role of the mystic utterance Om in* SIDDHARTHA. *In what ways does it foreshadow Siddhartha's spiritual progression? Is his relationship with it proactive, or reactive?*

2. *Herman Hesse's novels before* SIDDHARTHA *focused on alienated young men who rejected the cultures of their upbringings. However, these other novels did not feature the spiritual elements of* SIDDHARTHA. *How do the spiritual elements of* SIDDHARTHA *make it different from any other story of an alienated youth?*

3. SIDDHARTHA *is a love story in addition to the story of a spiritual quest. How do Siddhartha's romantic love for Kamala and his love for his son impact his spirituality? How does Siddhartha's spirituality, in turn, impact Kamala and his son?*

4. *Most literary scholars agree that* SIDDHARTHA *was prompted by Herman Hesse's fixation on Eastern spirituality. Is there a case to be made that* SIDDHARTHA *is designed to celebrate Eastern religion? Is Hesse's treatment of spirituality as relevant today as it was when he wrote the novel?*

5. SIDDHARTHA *concerns the quest for spiritual enlightenment, and by the end of it four characters have achieved this goal: Govinda, Gotama, Vasudeva, and Siddhartha. Is the enlightenment achieved by each of these characters the same? Why or why not? What distinctions and similarities exist between the paths these characters use to reach their final goal?*

Review and Resources

Quiz

1. Siddhartha's father is a Brahmin, which means he is a what?

    A. Policeman
    B. Religious leader
    C. Soldier
    D. Politician

2. What is the name of Siddhartha's best friend?

    A. Gotama
    B. Govinda
    C. Kamala
    D. Kamaswami

3. When Siddhartha joins the Samanas, what pleasant surprise does he find?

    A. That he has a brother
    B. That his own father was once a Samana
    C. That Govinda has also joined the Samanas
    D. That the Samanas have chosen to make Siddhartha their leader

4. In the course of his confrontational departure from the Samanas, how does Siddhartha silence their leader?

    A. By gazing at him hypnotically
    B. By wrestling with him and winning
    C. By criticizing the dress of the Samanas
    D. By threatening to tell Gotama about them

5. What does Govinda do when Siddhartha leaves the Samanas?

    A. Remains with the Samanas
    B. Returns to their home village
    C. Wanders to a river
    D. Accompanies Siddhartha

6. After learning the main tenets of Gotama's Eightfold Path, what does Siddhartha do?

    A. Questions Gotama privately about the specifics of his spiritual recommendations

    B. Acknowledges Gotama's beliefs as making up the one true faith

    C. Insists to Govinda that they leave immediately

    D. Attempts to return to the Samanas, but fails to locate their whereabouts

7. Why does Gotama seem to believe he is qualified to be a spiritual leader?

    A. He has read every spiritual text in existence

    B. He was once the leader of the Samanas

    C. He has many followers

    D. He has attained Nirvana

8. When Siddhartha decides to leave Gotama's camp, what does Govinda do?

    A. Accompanies Siddhartha

    B. Stays with Gotama

    C. Appears unexpectedly, but doesn't recognize Siddhartha

    D. Returns to the Samanas

9. How does the ferryman first seem to Siddhartha?

    A. Bitter and lost

    B. Cringing and self-serving

    C. Contented and smiling

    D. Dazed and confused

10. On his approach to the city, Siddhartha is almost overcome by desire for what?

    A. A woman

    B. Kamaswami

    C. A home-cooked meal

    D. Alcoholic beverages

11. Soon after Kamala meets Siddhartha, what does she agree to trade a kiss for?

    A. A well-recited poem

    B. A well-sung song

    C. An amusing acrobatic trick

    D. A beautiful painting

12. Why does Kamala introduce Siddhartha to Kamaswami?

    A. So Siddhartha will have a friend in the city

    B. So Siddhartha can learn the ways of a merchant

    C. Kamaswami is the city's greatest spiritual leader

    D. So Siddhartha may fight a duel with him for the hand of Kamala

13. Siddhartha has a dream about Kamala's pet bird. In Siddhartha's dream, what is different about Kamala's bird?

    A. It has the head of a fish

    B. It is a different color

    C. It speaks in the voice of Govinda

    D. It is dead

14. Soon after his dream about Kamala's bird, Siddhartha retires to a pleasure garden. What does he do here?

    A. Encounters Govinda, who fails to recognize him

    B. Encounters Kamala and follows her into the woods

    C. Engages in sexual intercourse with Kamala

    D. Resolves to leave the city

15. During Siddhartha's second encounter with the river, what does he do when he sees his own reflection in the water?

    A. Asks it to teach him the nature of Nirvana

    B. Spits at it

    C. Flashes a big smile

    D. Fails to recognize himself

16. After Siddhartha falls asleep on the riverbank during his
     second encounter with the river, who does he awake to find?

     A.   Govinda, who fails to recognize him
     B.   Gotama, who fails to recognize him
     C.   Kamala, who Siddhartha fails to recognize
     D.   Kamaswami

17. When Siddhartha convinces the ferryman Vasudeva to teach
     him how to listen to the river, how does Vasudeva propose to
     train him?

     A.   Siddhartha will meet with Vasudeva once a day
     B.   Siddhartha will learn to swim in the river
     C.   Siddhartha will replace Vasudeva as the ferryman for
          one year, and Vasudeva will return periodically to
          check his progress
     D.   Siddhartha will live and work alongside Vasudeva

18. Early in his time spent learning from Vasudeva, what news
     does Siddhartha hear from a group of Buddhists?

     A.   The Samanas have declared war on Gotama's followers
     B.   The Samanas have disbanded
     C.   Gotama is dying
     D.   Gotama has attained a new and deeper level of Nirvana

19. What causes Kamala's death?

     A.   A disease
     B.   An accident
     C.   A snakebite
     D.   A natural disaster

20. When Siddhartha learns he has a son, what does he propose?

     A.   The son should follow Gotama
     B.   The son should live with Govinda
     C.   The son should live with Siddhartha at the river
     D.   The son should live in the city with Kamaswami

21. When Siddhartha's son steals Siddhartha's money, what does Siddhartha do?

    A. Follows him to the outskirts of the city, where the trail ends

    B. Spreads the word from town to town that his son is a shameful thief

    C. Declares to Vasudeva that his son is no longer a relation

    D. Takes him to the Samanas' camp, where he is forced to become an ascetic

22. Through what activity does Siddhartha achieve true Nirvana?

    A. Following the precepts of Gotama

    B. Listening to the teachings of the river

    C. Successfully recognizing Govinda

    D. Reluctantly welcoming his estranged son back into his life

23. After Siddhartha shows the signs of having attained Nirvana, what does Vasudeva do?

    A. Urges Siddhartha to teach his own son

    B. Sings and dances in celebration

    C. Leaves for the city, presumably to start a new life

    D. Leaves to die in the forest

24. When Siddhartha meets Govinda for the final time, what initially happens?

    A. Siddhartha fails to recognize Govinda

    B. Govinda fails to recognize Siddhartha

    C. Govinda reveals that he has recently attained Nirvana

    D. Govinda reveals that he has abandoned his quest for enlightenment

REVIEW & RESOURCES

25. At the end of the novel, how does Siddhartha share his experience of Nirvana with his old friend Govinda?

    A.   He has Govinda kiss his forehead

    B.   He makes Govinda wash his feet

    C.   He coaches Govinda to listen to the teachings of the river

    D.   He goes into the woods and leaves Govinda to be the next ferryman

Suggestions for Further Reading

BOULBY, MARK. *Hermann Hesse: His Mind and Art.* Ithaca, New York: Cornell University Press, 1967.

CASEBEER, EVAN. *Hermann Hesse.* New York: Warner Paperback, 1972.

MILECK, JOSEPH. *Hermann Hesse and His Critics: The Criticism and Bibliography of Half a Century.* New York: AMS Press, 1966.

SORRELL, WALTER. *Hermann Hesse: The Man who Sought and Found Himself.* London: Oswald Wolff, 1974.

STELZIG, EUGENE. *Hermann Hesse's Fictions of the Self: Autobiography and the Confessional Imagination.* Princeton, New Jersey: Princeton University Press, 1988.

ZIOLKOWSKI, THEODORE, ed. *Hesse: A Collection of Critical Essays.* Englewood Cliffs, New Jersey: Prentice Hall, 1973.

———, ed. *Hermann Hesse: Autobiographical Writings.* New York: Farrar, Strauss, and Giroux, 1972.

SparkNotes® Literature Guides